WIRED DIFFERENTLY

DRIFTAGAIN

EIGHT TRAITS OF SUPREMELY PURPOSEFUL PEOPLE

"Stop Drifting, Start Achieving."
-TODD SAYLOR

Testimonials for Todd Saylor and DriftAgain

In today's world of complacency and fear of competitiveness because of the possibility of failure, I find Todd Saylor's second book, Wired Differently: DriftAgain a promising glimpse of how our nation could restore itself once again. This collection of thoughts is a "punch in the face" to remind us that greatness comes from the willingness to fight and compete for the goals we have set before us.

My name is Lloy Ball. I am a four-time Olympian and a 2008 Gold Medal winner. I played 15 years professionally in Europe and am in the International Volleyball Hall of Fame. I own and run a successful youth sports program at the Ball Sports Academy. Just like my friend Todd Saylor, I too am Wired Differently! All winners are!

As a long-time competitor at the Olympic level, I find many parallels with Todd's process to make all aspects of a competition. These "Marks" as he calls them, allow him to identify, fight, and overcome the roadblocks we encounter in life just as we do on the playing field.

The mentorship that Todd received from his dad mimics my own upbringing. My father, Arnie Ball, also was a winning championship coach. His ability to show me how to challenge myself constantly is what pushed me to Olympic Gold Medal glory. My dad helped me identify the "Marks" on the court and off so that I understood the challenges that lay before me, and that I must prepare to fight for the "win" because in the real world, victory will simply not be given to you.

This book reminds me of what is needed to not just get through life but to WIN life. The willingness to work and compete at the highest and hardest level to defeat your "Mark" is the mantra with which Todd and DriftAgain drives me forward. I hope that after you read this book, you are inspired as I am to be Wired Differently.

- Lloy Ball, 4-time Olympian, 2008 Gold Medalist, NCAA All-American Owner/Director of Team Pineapple VBC and the Ball Sports Academy

Todd Saylor is authentic. In the years I have known him, both professionally and as a friend, he has exemplified the principles he shares…he truly does "say what he means, and lives what he says"! He has the energy of his convictions and those convictions are always to help, not hinder, anyone willing to elevate their thinking and living! I am very excited about the adventure Todd started in Wired Differently and is continuing with DriftAgain.

- Chuck Goodrich: Indiana State Representative and CEO of Gaylor Electric

Many people talk about success, but Todd Saylor is a living, breathing, purposeful example of it. I am so honored and proud of him and the remarkable work he's done with the Wired Differently brand. Rarely have I seen someone with so much passion and dedication to help people "get it"! DriftAgain is a powerful book that will show you exactly how to get what you want in life; just know that Todd's approach is going to show you how to get it…by being

Wired Differently! If you allow the content in this book to help you "Believe in, Prepare for, and Attack" your divinely inspired goals and dreams, no good thing will be withheld from you, my friend!

- Delatorro L. McNeal II: MS, CSP, Peak Performance Expert Global Convention Keynote Speaker, Best-selling Author & TV Personality

Since being gifted the book Wired Differently, my perspective on business and life has vastly improved. The book explains seven fulcrums on behavior and leveraging your favors. The one that stands out most, and which I believe anyone can incorporate into their life, is Fulcrum #2, Distance. "We are not separated by the efforts that we make, but by the distances we are willing to go." My translation is this: Effort will not complete the task, only completing the task will complete the task—go the Distance. This one principle has stayed with me and has shifted my mindset on all projects. Before committing to a "yes," I ask myself, am I willing to go the Distance?

In my life, being Wired Differently is making sure I conduct all my business with complete integrity, because at some point in the future, you'll need to leverage your connections capital. The ability to leverage favors will correlate directly to your reputation. Know that being successful requires "no talent." The decisions you make to show up, get up early, do the extra work, and serve others require no formal training, and are the result of putting WD knowledge to use so you can get the Edge. Wired Differently is not an expression or a label, but a way of life. If you are serious about serving others and winning, choose to live Wired Differently.

- Michael "Ninja Mike" Domaratius Entrepreneur

Todd was my high-school football coach, and it was obvious even back then in 1989 that he was a man on a mission in many different areas of life. Throughout the years I kept in touch with Todd because of the respect I had for him and the similarities in our respective businesses. It was no surprise when Todd decided to write a book and get his story out there. In fact, I was so impressed with his Wired Differently concept that I purchased the book for all of my young managers and sent a copy to our CEO/President, whom I report to directly. Todd has a way of relating real-world stories and applying them to many areas of life, not the least of which is the business world. Todd's Christian faith is a huge bonus in these life lessons and for me makes them more credible and impactful.

- Robb Getts: First Fleet, Director of Operations

Todd is more than a customer or a coworker or a boss or even a friend; he is an aggressively motivated individual who is deeply passionate about helping others. Todd is the reason my company doubled, then tripled in growth and stability. His book Wired Differently challenged and pushed me to learn about myself and my favors. I have benefitted greatly from Todd and his insights into not just the person but also their abilities, strengths, and weaknesses. I am grateful for Todd's interest in helping me grow as a person and business owner.

- Curtis Fowler: CEO, Owner of Temporary Employment of Xenial Tradesmen (TEXT) Electrical Engineer, Entrepreneur, Inventor

CONTENTS

This book is dedicated to my daughters: Courtnee Dawn Saylor, Kendra Saylor Scharite, Kara Nicole Saylor. Although my daughters are clearly Wired Differently, their presence was crucial during the formative years of my developing Wired Differently actions, my Drift, and my DriftAgain. I'm grateful for their love, support, and forgiveness of the parenting process and my drive for success, which has been challenging for everyone. I love you ladies more than you can comprehend and I'm so very proud of you.

Love, Daddio

SPECIAL EDITION AUTHOR'S NOTE

Writing a book is hard work. When completing *DriftAgain: 8 Traits of Supremely Purposeful People Wired Differently* and wrapping things up, I wanted an image for the cover that would capture the essence of the book.

Seems simple enough. Then I got hit hard with Covid. Despite that, I had to push ahead with life, work, and completing the book. One final detail was the cover image, and the photo shoot happened the day after the end of my three-week illness and quarantine. I still wasn't a hundred percent but I forced myself to get the photos taken. My team and I picked an image for the cover that everyone thought was perfect.

But interestingly enough, I kept a second photo in mind, one that I almost chose as the cover and frankly, that I liked as much. Why did I not opt for this second image?

In the book, I explained the process of the photo shoot and here we are some five months after the release of this book and I'm proud to announce that we've sold over 5000 copies, a remarkable achievement. But as I track sales, I'm still wondering why God kept me from not posting that second photo as the book cover?

That image is similar to the one from the original cover—me striding barefoot through the surf, completely soaked, my pants rolled up and the ocean surging past my legs—the embodiment of being ferociously purposeful as I walk toward the distant horizon.

I love that cover of this first book just as I love every word printed inside. I love the book's message from page one to the end. That magnificent cover captures the excitement and enthusiasm of *DriftAgain* and its proclamation of Supremely Purposeful traits.

The second image showed me walking toward dark storm clouds, which was why I didn't use it. When *DriftAgain* was published, I felt that we as a nation were turning the corner on Covid and that things in America were looking up. I wanted a more upbeat image for the cover and that was why I selected that first photo.

But with January 2021, the country was still embroiled in many complications: vaccine debates, mask mandates, rising prices, supply-chain issues, school and child care challenges, and a budget deficit crisis. Things were not getting better as we had hoped. In fact, it appears like our downward slide continues. We're left asking, What's next for our country? What's next in this world?" For those of us who are *Wired Differently*, we're wondering how could we overcome these challenges if not for our Supremely Purposeful traits?

How do we face the storm head on?

How do we survive in these times?

To answer those questions, I wanted a different cover image for a special edition of *DriftAgain: 8 Traits of Supremely Purposeful People*. I wanted this alternative cover to show me as that Supremely Purposeful person, for I would be dripping wet, walking head on into the storm but with a breath of sunshine beckoning forward, a promise of hope and bounty if we challenge ourselves to press through these moments of crises.

You must take on such moments no matter how they manifest themselves: as a *Supremely Purposeful* attitudinal disorder; or if you're conquering your demons; conquering your personal disasters; conquering this world and its way of beating us all down.

With that in mind, I've penned this special note for this the special edition of Facing the Storm, *Wired Differently, DriftAgain: 8 Traits of Supremely Purposeful People.*

If you're one of those people facing the storms, this book is for you. I want you to be prepared for what it did for me and for what it's done for my growing audience of readers. If you're one of those people, I'm certain that this alternative cover speaks to you as it spoke to me.

We are not perfect and as such, we will *DriftAgain* and when we do, remember to face the storm. Walk head on into the storm, your head held forward, trudging relentlessly forward because you are *Wired Differently*, propelled by unique forces, drawing upon the traits of being Supremely Purposeful.

You will conquer.

You will lead on.

Before you read this special author's edition, let me share these four points to give you the understandings of leadership guidance and how successful people become successful differently.

What are these four points that successful leaders do?

1. They surround themselves with quality relationships. People who are uplifting in turn motivate like-minded people who are thinking differently. They are willing to face the storm, going together in the same direction in a manner that makes others better people as well.

2. Successful people have "attitudinal disorder." They possess a great attitude even in the worst of times. This attitudinal disorder forces them to turn into the prevailing storm, their heads held forward.

3. Successful people equip others. They learn to take care of themselves, building positive attributes so they can then equip others to charge into the storm as a team.

4. And finally you must LEAD , lead yourself to grow. Lead yourself to go forward INTO THE STORM. Lead yourself to get up in the morning, ready to go. Lead yourself to small wins. Lead yourself to big wins. Lead yourself to lead...lead, lead, lead. I once attended a talk by the acclaimed leadership coach and author John Maxwell who told us, "All successful people lead and leadership is the beginning of everything, all things that rise and fall become of leadership. Everything in this world needs leadership, which is inherent in all things." Somebody in the back of the room asked, "John, what do you mean by everything rises and falls with leadership?" John acknowledged the question, took a sip of water, slowly adjusted himself, looked at him and the entire crowd, then answered, "Everything rises and falls with leadership. Everything in this entire world rises and falls with leaders."

Facing the storm is about the leadership of you "facing the storm." It's about moving forward no matter what. This special edition has a different cover to help you understand where you are in this world right now. I want you to realize that this book will help you move through the storms in your life. It will *Wire* you *Differently*. This book will help you face the storms, move through them, and understand how any crisis can be overcome with a *Supremely Purposeful* mindset.

I'm grateful that you chose this book, that you're one who considers themselves as one of *8 Traits of Supremely Purposeful People* to avoid the *DriftAgain*. You can do this thing called life as *Wired Differently* as we face the storm. Thank you for letting me speak to you as we face our storms together and thank you for being a leader.

Todd Saylor

FOREWORD

I have known Todd for nearly 30 years and always admired his "motor," for it never slowed down, and he was always up for a new challenge. There are two areas in my life I will eternally be grateful to Todd for as he personally challenged me to be *Wired Differently*.

1) A desire to study God's Word. When we were in Bible study together, I wanted to make sure I knew just as much about the scripture passages as did Todd.

2) Chapter 1 of *Wired Differently*, "The Drift." For the first 57 years of my life, I was not what I would call a risk taker; I always played it safe. Always very safe and very conservative in everything I did. That in itself is not a bad thing, but it kept me from thinking what else is out there.

As a result, I got stuck in the "Land of Quo." Todd defined this as "another term for the status quo but a bigger version of your surroundings and where you exist." Throughout the book, Todd challenged me: "If you're someone who's just stuck in life and afraid to make a move...here's a question for you, 'Do you want to be average?' If you're *Wired Differently* and proud of it, and if your answer is 'No,' then let's take this journey together." Those words challenged my family and me to begin a new journey of our own. We had for years wanted to move from Indiana to Florida to be closer to my wife's family but had always been afraid to make the move. In 2019 we put a plan in action to leave the "Land of Quo." We sold our home, I quit my job of nearly 36 years, and left behind numerous friends and the church we helped establish in 1992. Since arriving in Florida, I've landed a fantastic job, my wife has been able to work from home, our high-school daughter has settled in nicely, plus our two adult children have also moved here and we found a wonderful church. Thank you, Todd, for listening to me and helping me get out of my "Land of Quo."

- Doug Tuckerman: Human Resources Manager, Detwiler Farm Market

INTRODUCTION

The year was 1977. I was 12 when my family moved to Angola, Indiana. We'd just left Hudson, Michigan, where my father had been the head football coach and the winningest high-school coach in the nation. What was about to transpire became the most defining moment in my formative *Wired Differently* journey.

That evening, my dad insisted that I go with him to watch Fremont High School play a larger school from across the state. Since I played football, not basketball, I had no desire to watch the game, let alone a team from another school.

"Dad," I protested, "why do I need to go? I don't care about them or basketball."

My dad replied, "Come on, Butch. I want you to see this. Get in the car and let's go."

I had no real choice but to obey; he was, after all, my dad, and I respected him more than anyone. I first put on my Angola Hornets t-shirt. As we drove across the snowy road toward the Fremont High gym, I couldn't help wondering what the big deal was. We arrived late, so the only place to sit was on a bleacher right along the court. When we walked in, it was obvious to the crowd that my dad and I were, if not the bad guys, then definitely from another school. As we made our way past the cheerleaders and the Eagle mascot to our seats, we had to endure the kind of taunts you might expect from high schoolers. You know, like, "Down in front!" and "Go back to Angola, this is Eagle country!"

As we sat, my dad said, "Never mind them, son. We have work to do."

"Work?" I thought we were here to watch basketball. "What kind of work?"

"I want you to watch these Fremont Eagle boys play this game."

"Why?" I asked, confused.

"We're here for a purpose. Just focus on the game."

The Fremont team was a rural squad with a small roster. The next forty minutes flew by as I watched these farm boys battle against a much larger team.

I didn't see a lot of great basketball moves but I did witness the Fremont squad play with amazing, relentless hustle. They sprinted, dove, leapt, screamed, fought, and bled as they pressed the other team. I had never seen anything like this in my life. A heroic, spellbinding, remarkable display of determination, of going-the-distance efforts that they kept up to the very last second of the game. They'd played their guts out and practically collapsed with exhaustion when the final buzzer sounded just as they scored the winning point.

On the drive home, my father looked at me. "So, Son, why do you think I brought you here? What did you learn?"

It seemed like a trick question; my dad was known for his trick questions. "Dad, I'm not sure. I guess I learned how to play basketball. Do whatever it takes to help my team. Be relentless. Not care what others think but instead focus on the game and never quit until the end no matter what."

My father pulled over to the side of the road. He put the car in park and calmly regarded me. "Not quite, son. It's not just about how I want you to play basketball or any other game..." He paused a beat, then said:

———

*"It's how I want you to live your entire life." -**Tom Saylor***

———

CHAPTER ONE

THE DRIFTAGAIN

*"Look for the Drift, Prepare for the DriftAgain." -**Todd Saylor***

The following happened on a March afternoon in 2015. I was at the wheel of my new BMW and had stopped on the Cortez Bridge that connects Anna Marie Island to Manatee County, south of St. Petersburg, Florida. The center of the bridge, called a bascule, had been raised to allow large boats to pass underneath. I was the first car in line along the eastern side of the bridge and when the bascule lowered flush into position, I began to cross.

A similar line of cars headed our direction over the narrow bridge. Then incredibly, a Lincoln Continental drifted from behind the others, veered into my lane, and accelerated.

What was he doing? My brain immediately focused on my dilemma. I was helpless, trapped by a line of cars behind me, the guardrail to my right, and oncoming traffic on my left. Staring in wonder, I watched this guy as he gained speed toward me. In those short seconds, my mind fixed on the stark realization that there was nothing I could do to protect myself from this drifting car. I slowed gradually to prevent a pile-up behind me, put my car in neutral, and braced for impact.

The Lincoln didn't slow as if the driver hadn't even seen me. When his car collided into mine head on, the concussion slammed me against the seat harness.

In the abrupt aftermath, there was a quiet, surreal moment as if time seemed to have stood still. For my part, I was rattled and in sudden pain. My back and legs were strangely hurt.

I gazed over the crumpled hood of my car at the smashed front end of the Lincoln. The driver—the only passenger—was slumped over the steering wheel. Gathering my thoughts, I climbed out of my sedan and made my way to the other car as it remained idling. Conflicting emotions churned through me: relief that I wasn't seriously injured; a humanitarian concern for the other driver; and bewilderment at this outrageous situation.

I leaned through his open passenger window, not certain if I was going to give him first aid or confront him. A medicinal brewery smell poured from the Lincoln and that explained it all.

Then he jerked up, suddenly wide awake, glanced about at all the damage he'd caused, and scowled at me, asking, "Where the hell did you come from?" He then groped under his dashboard as if searching for a weapon.

Looking him in the eye, I warned, "Don't even think about it."

Then he abruptly put his car into reverse, racing backwards like he was in *The Dukes of Hazzard.* I hopped back into my car and as wrecked as it was, I gave chase. When he cleared the bridge backwards, he tried to swerve into a one-eighty but careened against a guardrail and stalled out, teetering on the sidewalk and the ocean embankment.

The Bradenton Beach Police arrived. I got arrested for causing the accident, but witnesses testified on my behalf and I was released. The police detained the other guy and handed him over to the Manatee County Sheriff's Office; they arrested and charged him with DUI and other violations.

Even though I wasn't at fault, I kept replaying the wreck in my head. When you've been in an accident like this, you have a hard time letting it go and can't help but contemplate over what you might've done differently to mitigate or prevent the accident.

It was obvious that the other driver was under the influence and I pondered that. His drinking problems were a symptom that something in his life was seriously out of whack. I'm positive that it wasn't in his career plans to become a reckless alcoholic and flush his money and reputation down the toilet. The problems that led to his drinking had caused him to drift away from his life's path and allowed his vehicle to drift into my life's path.

Drift.

My mind wrapped tight around that word. I was familiar with Drift. It's that constant slide into the *Land of Quo*, that place of mediocrity and frustrated ambitions, and this particular drift had gone completely rogue.

This made me think about why I was on the Cortez Bridge that particular afternoon. Just as that other driver was on the bridge because of his Drift, I was there because of mine.

For the last five years, I'd been working extra hard trying to again realign my businesses. I was still dealing with the aftermath of a big downturn from the recession and had lost many clients. By putting in extra time and assuming more risks, I had managed to crawl back to higher ground. In the middle of that effort, I was trying to sell my company. On top of all that, I had to cover some difficult investments and business deals that had soured. If that wasn't enough bad news on my plate, a business associate had absconded with $250,000, and that brought its own set of expensive legal hassles and pain.

Financially, I felt squeezed really hard. To recover from this mess, I was flying all over the country, working deals, putting in too much time and travel. I had few weekends off. It was a torrid pace, but I felt that I had no choice if I were to keep my business, lifestyle, and hope.

What does this have to do with the Drift? Or the car wreck?

The reason had to do with my oldest daughters, Courtnee and Kendra. Earlier, during one of my rare weekends home, my wife Traci pulled me aside. "Todd, I need to talk to you. Courtnee and Kendra have been telling me it's like they have two different dads. They feel forgotten because they haven't received the same attention you've given their youngest sister. You're one kind of dad to them and another kind of dad to Kara. Not only that, you've become distant to me as well."

Traci's remarks struck a nerve. I knew exactly what she was getting at because I'd been there before. For the record, I don't believe I was a bad dad. What pained my oldest daughters was that what they weren't getting was me, meaning I wasn't making time for them. My wife certainly felt the same about our relationship.

When the girls were young, there was a five-year period when I had allowed myself to focus on my business at the expense of my family. At the time, I had rationalized the situation by telling myself what I was doing was on everyone's behalf. All this hard work represented my sacrifice, and my family would reap the material benefits. But my wife and kids didn't see it that way. What I was communicating was that the business was more important to me than they were. My actions strained my relationship with my wife and my relationships with Courtnee and Kendra. When I got through those very trying years, I made it a point to turn my attention back to them, and for the distress that I've caused, I truly apologize.

Now here I was, returning to that same stagnant place in our relationships. How had this happened?

I knew exactly how. Before the crash today, I'd been at the gym and just before I was about to head home, I received a call from a client. He wanted to discuss some business. Even though I'd promised my daughters that I was heading straight home to spend time with them, I changed my plans because of the client. The sad part was that his request wasn't urgent. There was no reason I couldn't have told him that we would meet tomorrow. But I was so focused on work that I'd brushed aside all other considerations, even time for my two oldest, again.

That realization curdled within me. I thought about all the family events I'd missed, plus the sports functions, the celebrations. Like it or not, I had been an absentee dad and the emotional void was a symbolic message to my daughters.

My thoughts circled back to the car wreck. That driver's Drift had consequences not just for him, but for me as well.

I realized that Drift has collateral damage.

During the last five years I'd been so focused on my business that I hadn't even noticed the Drift as it affected my family life.

I was aware of the time I was spending at work. But like ... rationalized my decision. I was making big sacrifices for the sake of my family and a price of these sacrifices was my time away from them. That was the nature of my work. After all, I was a busy entrepreneur at the helm of several operations, each worth millions of dollars.

What other choice did I have? If I opted for a 9-to-5 job that would give me time at night and on the weekends, where would I be in twenty years? Living in a cramped house, pinching pennies, clipping coupons because money was tight. I'd seen too many guys who ended up in that difficult position. I wouldn't have the financial wherewithal to buy my kids nice cars or send them to a good college. I wasn't putting in all this extra work just for me. My wife and daughters would live the good life thanks to my efforts.

Well, that's how I justified my decision. The problem was that I didn't comprehend at the time that the Drift doesn't just affect us, but those around us as well. Our coworkers. Our family. Even some random stranger on a bridge.

For the Drift has two components:
- Your pain.
- Collateral damage—the pain you cause others because of your selfish Drift.

In trying to fix my business and financial problems I'd been so caught up in my pain that I didn't see the collateral damage my actions were causing. Or that I even had options to prevent the Drift. Hell, I didn't even see that I had *Drifted Again*.

When Traci told me how distant I had gotten from my oldest daughters and her, especially—*how far I had allowed us to Drift from each other*—I decided to make it up to them.

Then the day's chain of arbitrary events came together. The driver and his problems that led to alcoholism. His decision to drive across the bridge and then impulsively, and in complete disregard for anyone else, to drift into my lane and accelerate.

Me and the years of taking my oldest daughters for granted. The anxiety I had caused them and my beautiful wife. My decision to spend time with them that day, then to change plans at the last minute by deciding to meet a client, which led to me crossing the bridge at that exact moment, and the other driver and I converging our drifts.

The resulting head-on collision became a metaphor for the collateral damage caused by the two drifts.

———

"You can learn a lot from your mistakes when you aren't busy denying them."
- Oscar Auliq-Ice

———

From this story it's obvious why I'm discussing my Drift again, which is such an important and singular concept that I've identified it as one word: *DriftAgain*. If it happened to me, it can happen to anyone. But people don't see my *DriftAgain*, they instead see my accomplishments as a straight and smooth road toward success.

DriftAgain is the biggest killer of any *Wired Differently* person.

DriftAgain is actually the number-one trait of Supremely Purposeful people, and we must prepare for the *DriftAgain*.

For *DriftAgain* hobbles if not cripples you if you're not prepared for it. You must be respectful of the pain you can cause because of the *DriftAgain*. *DriftAgain,* which can manifest itself as kryptonite to we who are *Wired Differently*, happens quietly and easily as you fall back on the familiar until it confronts you head on, on a bascule, leaving people in stalled traffic gawking in wonder, perhaps even suffering collaterally from your *DriftAgain*.

I own and manage a multimillion-dollar HCM company and as many as fourteen other entities that are leaders in their industry. My financial and entrepreneurial success has allowed me countless opportunities to discuss spirituality and business through a multitude of venues: radio, social media, and as a public speaker, and most recently my podcast on iTunes and Spotify called the Wired Differently Experience.

People see my blessings and they ask: *"Todd, how do you do it?"*

In truth, I haven't done anything worthy of a Nobel Prize. I haven't cured cancer. I haven't found an answer to social injustice.

But I know why people ask me that question. What they want to know is how did I rise above the mediocre? How did I prevail over life's uncertain challenges? How am I really different?

In my first book, *Wired Differently*, I answered those questions and shared the concepts of how you and I are Wired Differently in pursuit of owning who we are and persevering after what we want.

Since then, I've become more appreciative of that force that pulls relentlessly against us, the *DriftAgain*. Sure, we can acknowledge it, thinking that by recognizing its presence, we can control it. But the truth is that the *DriftAgain* is constant and real. You alone are the enabler of the *DriftAgain* by your quiet acquiescence of life's compromises, by harboring the hubris that you're always on the right path, that you've mastered what caused you to Drift in the first place. As I illustrated in my example of the events leading to the collision, I was convinced that I was doing the proper thing by grinding away at my business when in fact, my family life was going off the rails.

This caused me to probe deeper into what it means to be *Wired Differently*. As I studied what it takes to overcome the Drift, I realized that the key to this process is that we must become *Supremely Purposeful* and control the *DriftAgain*.

That was an astounding discovery. I thought my success was that I was *Wired Differently*, which definitely explains why successful people are indeed successful.

But there's another aspect beyond that, which is, how do successful people prevail? It's that they're *Supremely Purposeful* in their pursuit of life, its opportunities, its bounty.

For you to understand what it takes to be *Supremely Purposeful* and to control the *DriftAgain*, you must first know how to be *Wired Differently*, which means to understand its foundational concepts. Let's begin by discussing:

The Drift: The constant shifting of our path away from where we should be going. This shift is the result of our compromises, both large and small, that delude us into thinking that these decisions are for our ultimate good. Then we look up from what we're doing, and we see that we're way off course and not at all heading in the direction of our goal. If the Drift is taking you from your path, then where are you headed? The Drift does indeed have a destination, which is the:

Land of Quo: My term for the status quo but a bigger version of your surroundings and where you exist. Often, we exist as drones in this "Land of Quo" where we accept the boundaries and limitations given to us. As a word of caution, the Land of Quo is no abstract concept. The Land of Quo has gravity. It pulls at you constantly, lulling you into complacency, deluding you with conceit and a false sense of comfort, and making you accept being average.

Favor: Any talent; a resource you might have developed; an experience that gave you a unique insight. Don't forget to count setbacks as favors because they can motivate you with more determination than does success. Within this broader definition of favor, we have what I call a "Favor Forward," a confronted weakness. *You can never rise above the level of your greatest weakness,* so why not make the recognition of your weakness, a Favor?

Fulcrum: A principle, a fundamental requisite premise, the base or foundation on which you pivot or hoist and lever a favor upon. It is the foundation and tipping point of action. This leveraging of your favor is what turns inaction into action. For example, the "Mind" is the fulcrum upon which you leverage your favor of "Work ethic." You concentrate actions to turn on that fulcrum of "Mind."

MIND:

"Success is a condition, not a position."

Being Wired Differently starts with the Mind. The thought processes, your consciousness—your Mind—controls how you perceive the world and respond. We can control our actions. Repeated actions build into habits and wire our brain to act accordingly. We do the reps to strengthen our habits which rewire our minds to live Wired Differently.

DISTANCE:

"We are not separated by the efforts that we make, but by the distances we are willing to go."

Distance is the measure of your commitment to reach your goal. Achieving our goals is more than effort, it's pushing that effort to new limits. When we set goals, we have to tell ourselves that we're ready to do everything possible to reach them. Remember, a fulcrum is what your favor pivots around. This leveraging of your favor is what turns inaction into action. In the case of Distance, you leverage favor for gain, and this commitment is more than effort.

FIGHT:

"Three things in life you must do. Breathe, eat, and fight."

Life is struggle. You're either fighting against circumstances or against an opponent. It might be on an athletic field or in business. You're going to want something, or someone will be keeping it from you. Or someone will try to take what you have. Or you could be attacked. Whatever the case, no one else is going to engage in that fight for you.

EXECUTION:

"You can't execute a plan if you don't have one."

Execution is putting into action your plan, which means you must have a plan. And a plan needs a goal, an end state, what you're working for and toward. But a plan, no matter how well-crafted or thorough, will be no more than a collection of ideas without putting them into action, meaning *Execution*.

EDGE:

"Your edge comes from the favor of being wired differently."

An edge is what sets you apart. Suppose you're up against someone bigger; your edge is that you'll work harder, become nimbler. What about against someone with deeper pockets? Then you'll work smarter.

ATTACK:

"The way you train is the way you'll live!"

To attack is to exploit opportunities by claiming the initiative. Be courageous. Be daring. Make the decision and go. Execute your plans through the three A's: Attitude, Action, Attack.

Your SALE:

"The message that is received is more important than your wisdom, efforts, or actions."

It's not enough that you succeed; it's how you succeed. How did you get others to cooperate? Through persuasion, but what kind? Was it through Manipulation or through Motivation? Did you go for the Win-Win where all parties felt that they got a good deal?

Inventory: Taking stock of what favors you have and how they can be used to your advantage. It you were stranded on a desert island you'd inventory your supplies and resources to survive. The same is true in regular life.

Leverage: The act of using the favors that you apply against a fulcrum. An example would be the effort of taking night classes to expand your knowledge of a necessary subject.

Leadership Palette: The skills, knowledge, and experience that you draw from to be an effective leader. These skills include communication, decisiveness, creativity, motivating, delegating, and other areas of leadership gifts.

Fear Exercise: The action of mind-conditioning by recognizing fears or apprehensions in your character and embracing them by doing exercises to conquer them. As an example, how do you conquer your fear of public speaking? By joining a theater group. Through such exercises, you learn to identify and confront your fears, thereby robbing them of their power.

DriftAgain: Recognizing and admitting that the very *Drift* that has consumed you once will be a lifelong hindrance that you need to be aware of and on the watch for.

Land of Quo Pro: The most highly successful, sometimes even famous, people who are stuck in success and wealth, remain unhappy because of type casting and are yet not willing to leave their Pro "Land of Quo."

Attitudinal Disorder: The propensity to react to crises with actionable *Differently* behavior.

Neuroplasticity: The ability of your brain to change its neural structure in response to experience.

Supremely Purposeful: The crystal-clear mindset that drives a ferocious focus on your precise objective or object.

When you've recognized that you're *Wired Differently*, to leverage those favors, to fight the *DriftAgain*, to stay out of the Land of Quo, to eliminate collateral damage, you must learn to be *Supremely Purposeful*. Remember, do you want to be average?

The answer better still be *NO!*

So let's GO! And—do this thing called life, together!

CHAPTER TWO

THE MARK

"Find your Mark, then use it, then really use it!" -**Todd Saylor**

Those of us who want to get ahead embrace the fact that we're *Wired Differently.* We recognize that we must leverage our Favors against Fulcrums to overcome life's challenges and reach success. Three of those Favors are the *Distance,* the *Fight,* and the *Edge.* With *Distance,* that is the measure of the commitment to reach our goal. In the *Fight* we acknowledge that conflict and action are necessary to gain a favorable position in pursuit of your goals. Likewise, the *Edge* is the process of how you leverage your *Tenacity* and *Work Ethic.*

We don't pursue our goals in a vacuum. We live in a world where we must compete because the customer can only choose one vendor, not everyone can come in first, and not everyone can be the best.

What helps us sharpen our *Edge* for the *Fight* is to direct our actions against one person, whom I call the Mark, defining them as something I've "marked" for identification. What the Mark does for me is that the competition is no longer an abstract concept.

The competition is now pegged to a Mark, that Mark now has a face and, equally important, that Mark is the measure I use to accomplish specific goals.

How does having a Mark help you realize your success?

- Beating your Mark satisfies your need to win. We humans have caveman brains and we're hard-wired to fight in order to survive, and if we fight, then we must win. Winning brings an invigorating feeling of triumph and that feeling carries over to building confidence and our sense of self-worth.
- Competing against your Mark creates the motivation for improving your performance. We want to beat the Mark, which plays into our desire to win.
- Competition brings out our best work because we're drawing on our maximum potential. Having a Mark raises the bar of what we expect from ourselves.
- Competing against a Mark opens your eyes to new possibilities and forces you to be creative.
- Competing against a Mark brings focus in our efforts to be *Supremely Purposeful*. In the desire and follow-through to win, all distractions fall away, and we will not *DriftAgain*.
- A worthy Mark knows that someone else is nipping at their heels. They fought to be leader of the pack so they're well aware that if they stumble, someone else will run right by. Consequently, the Mark is always fine-tuning their efforts and to beat them, you must tap into a deeper commitment— remember the Fulcrum *the Distance*?—that will produce a higher level of measured performance.

- Competition against a Mark attracts opportunity. Because of your effort you stand out and that forces others in your field to take notice. Just in wanting to compete, you've already elbowed your way past most of the also-rans and are ready to rumble with the few determined who remain.

Your Mark can be anyone. We might see a historical figure as a Mark because we know what trials and travails they had to overcome. Or the Mark could be a famous athlete or someone else acknowledged as a champion in their field.

But the best kinds of Mark are personal rivals. They're aware of the competition between the two of you and this brings psychological stakes into play that can be more important than any award or prize.

Think of famous rivalries. In business we saw Steve Jobs versus Bill Gates. In sports, we saw Larry Bird versus Magic Johnson. These contests brought tremendous dividends to the rest of us. For Jobs and Gates, there was the technological one-upmanship that inspired electronic innovations which changed the world. For Bird and Johnson, these rivalries were grudge matches that exemplified athletic competition at its most rewarding.

These matchups showed that interpersonal relationships can have a substantial impact on motivation, which demonstrates how rivalry can boost performance far above that of normal competition. For example, when a task affects one's self-evaluation, people are more competitive with friends than with strangers. What is brought into action is the psychological element that raises the personal stakes of the contest. It's no secret that a great motivator is the pain of being bested by someone you know.

Subconsciously, what the people did in the above example was establish a Mark. A rival brought focus to their efforts and motivated them into achieving higher performance. At the same time, you will soon, if not already, be someone else's Mark. So don't ever be complacent.

———

*"When you eclipse the Mark that you seek, then you'll become the Mark which is sought." -****Todd Saylor***

———

The year was 1996. My sales team had just arrived in Phoenix, Arizona, and we were headed to the world-renowned Biltmore hotel and resort for our national meeting. I was excited as I was in the running for the national top sales award, my first shot at the accolade.

The entire sales force had gathered for the corporate celebration. Besides the fact I was in the running for the company's top award, this was the first time I was to meet my competitive nemesis, Jerry Vogel. The guy was one of the titans in the business and even claimed to have invented the model for the Professional Employer Organization, known in the industry as a PEO. He was well situated for the same award as I was, especially as he hailed from New York, the financial capital of America, whereas to him, I was from podunk Angola, Indiana. Despite our many differences in circumstances, he was my Mark. I was determined to end his run as the legend in the business and claim his title as top salesman.

He and I finally met in the lobby of the corporate office where we got through the fake pleasantries that we were glad to be on the same team and all that. We were rivals and he knew it. And like I explained earlier, having a rival as a Mark brings an intense psychological thrust to the competition. It wasn't enough that I beat him in sales, I had to let him know that I was the company lead dog. Please understand that these were private thoughts which were never spoken aloud. But whenever we met in whatever capacity, he would have to acknowledge to himself that he wasn't going anywhere unless he was looking at my behind.

At our brief encounter I overheard that the next morning he would be in the hotel gym for his 6:00 AM cardio training. I filed that nugget of info away to use in my plan to knock him off balance.

I arrived at the gym at 5:00 AM. Back then my plans about myself were on an epic scale, as they still are today. It's something I inherited from my dad. He would arrange for events to unfold in an epic manner for maximum dramatic effect and would share stories of the amazing, almost unbelievable things that had happened in his life. As kids, we grew up soaking up every word of every tall tale that he told us.

He had actually convinced me that Indians raised him for the first five years of his life. The way he explained this was that as a baby, during a family hunting trip to a reservation he had fallen out of the back of a truck. I never questioned why my grandparents hadn't gone back to find him. My younger brother saw right through my dad's fable and tried to convince me why it couldn't possibly be true. But I preferred to hold tight to my dad's version because his story sounded so epic, and I wanted my life to be one of epic stories.

Because of the effect those stories had on my psyche I nurtured a desire to make my personal stories epic as well. When I went after something I was motivated to make the fight epic, and this morning's cardio attack on Jerry was going to be no different.

When I got to the gym, I did a quick circuit with weights and by 5:30 I was on the treadmill, waiting for Jerry to show up and start his run. When he finally arrived, I'd already been on the treadmill for thirty minutes. Since I had unplugged the other treadmills, he had no choice but to climb on the one adjacent to mine. As I was already covered in sweat and breathing moderately, he knew that I'd been exercising a while but didn't know for how long.

Jerry understood what was up between us. I'd arranged the situation to show that when it came to working out, he was a novice compared to me. To claim the edge over me he'd have to catch up, plus give a good showing especially as he was fresher.

When he was warmed up, he advanced his tread meter speed to 5. Right away I moved my speed to 5.5. For the next ten minutes we cruised at a steady cadence, him at 5 and me at 5.5. When he bumped up to 5.5 to match my pace, I immediately countered by going to 6.

Jerry left his speed at 5.5 for another twenty minutes. For my part, I was starting to feel some real pain, but I wasn't going to show this to Jerry. It was clear that he was going to try and out-distance me to gain the psychological advantage of his experience, using pacing and stamina versus my youth and quick power.

When I realized this, I settled in for the long haul as I was not going to be the first to quit. Never! I would pass out before that happened. Jerry had to get the message that I wasn't going away. What fueled my determination was that I felt that I deserved the top sales award and all the money and prestige that came with it.

Suffice it to say Jerry was also a warrior and so this unspoken contest of ours settled into a grueling race. Even though we had not exchanged a word about this duel, we both knew that the last one off his treadmill would be the champion.

Minute after minute, we kept pounding away. My side began to cramp and my legs to burn. Every breath became an effort. This race had moved past the realm of an athletic contest and into an ordeal of torture.

My mind shrank around the effort. Nothing else mattered. I told myself that everything else in my life, no matter how precious—my health, my hard-earned money, my family—wouldn't mean a thing if I didn't beat Jerry. It wasn't that I was pretending, I was completely invested in this reality.

I told myself, *Todd, this race against Jerry has become the defining moment in your life. If you lose to Jerry, you lose everything. You will never again have this opportunity to claim what is yours. If you pull up short, you will carry this defeat for the rest of your life. You lose and you are destined to abject poverty and your family will desert you for giving up.*

This is it, Todd. If you truly believe in yourself, prove it. Beat Jerry.

No doubt many of you are reading this, thinking, Todd, you're being ridiculous. You make things harder than they need to be.

In response, I will tell you, that *YES*, I am being ridiculous, and *YES*, I do make things harder for myself than necessary. But that's my motivational secret and a trait of being *Wired Differently*. In my mind I want to be epic in action in all endeavors, large and small.

You don't need to be a professional athlete to demonstrate a professional's embrace of combativeness and excellence. Professional athletes, gifted as they are, are no better at their craft than you are at yours or I am at mine.

At one time, I was such a high-level athlete. I understand the passion and mental drive they bring to their game and if you're *Wired Differently*, you must do likewise.

An hour and a half after he had started, Jerry stepped off the treadmill. I could tell by the look of exhaustion on his face that he had put forth his best effort. But just to show him, I nonchalantly bumped my treadmill speed to level 7 and continued until he left the room.

Then I threw up.

However, I had beat my Mark, one on one in personal competition. I had captured the edge. That year I became the top national salesman, then for two more consecutive years before being promoted to national sales director.

In that treadmill duel with Jerry Vogel, I had put everything on the line and because of my epic effort, I kept my family and averted abject poverty. Building on the momentum of that victory, I sold my company stock and started my own venture while searching for the next Mark to motivate me for the next epic push.

I owe my good and dear friend Jerry so much for his Mark and then his subsequent mentorship in life. RIP Jerry Vogel. I love you; see you in heaven.

What is your Mark?

M—stands for Jerry, *My Jerry*.

A—Awareness

R—Run your ass off.

K—Kall it, then *Krush it!*

———

"I have been up against tough competition all my life. I wouldn't know how to get along without it." - **Walt Disney**

———

CHAPTER THREE

THE EGO

*"I love to talk about my favorite subject: Me." -***Todd Saylor**

I despise this chapter. I've pondered and written it several times but yet it continues to feel indulgent and misleading. How to write about Ego and not make it *egocentric*? And more about other people? Hold that thought and here we go…

Long ago, I learned to appreciate the power of confidence. No, I don't believe that I was born with an overabundance of confidence and will admit I had very little confidence as a child. But I did see how the power of confidence manifested itself in my parents and in my leaders at school. I grew to recognize the authority and deference that it brought to them. I was clearly drawn to the commanding presence that allowed my parents, coaches, and other leaders to get things done and done on their terms. Conclusion: You need to love and believe in yourself. You need an Ego!

Which brings me to why I titled this chapter *The Ego*.

Remember though, *An Ego without Empathy will sabotage you.*

In our society, acting on your *Ego* labels you as arrogant. Self-centered. An egomaniac. A schemer. Unscrupulous. Untrustworthy. Shallow. Selfish. Petty. Vain.

But ask psychologists to explain someone acting on their *Ego* and a more nuanced and clearer picture emerges about such a person. Here is what psychologists say about people who act on their *Ego*:

- Have a high concept of themselves.
- Possess mental toughness.
- Are risk takers.
- Seek and embrace challenges.
- Use challenges as opportunities for personal growth.
- Tend to succeed in what they pursue.

What people who act on their *Ego* are accused of most is that they're selfish. But is being selfish actually a bad thing? It's a fact of life that no one knows you as well as you know yourself, that you alone are ultimately responsible for your happiness and well-being.

———

"Selfish—a judgment readily passed by those who have never tested their own power of sacrifice." -George Eliot

———

One significant downside to being described as acting on your *Ego* is that despite the outward appearance of confidence, within themselves such individuals can lack self-esteem and are vulnerable to criticism. Of this, I am guilty as charged. My lack of confidence meant that I often felt left out or that I fell short of what was expected of me.

As I was gathering my thoughts for writing about *The Ego*, I realized that my favorite TV characters all had that power of confidence that I admired:

William Shatner as Denny Crane in *Boston Legal*.

Ted Danson as Sam "Mayday" Malone in *Cheers*.

Charlie Sheen as Charlie Harper in *Two and a Half Men*.

Matt LeBlanc as Joey Tribbiani in *Friends*.

What these characters had in common was their strong *Ego*.

———

The Ego, the I, the identity of self for any person.

———

The Ego is important because no one is invested in your well-being and success more than you are. This investment in yourself manifests itself upon those who depend on you—your family, your business, your teammates. You do well, they do well.

We recognize that acting on the *Ego* is a big part of reaching success, of being *Supremely Purposeful*. Having a strong *Ego* gives us the confidence to strive for things that others don't see and the fortitude to persevere through tough times because we know that our vision is true.

So how do we reconcile this with what we do for others?

Empathy, Ego, Balance

At this point, let me explain so we don't confuse ourselves. If we focus too much on the *Ego* and see our actions only as they affect us, then we act without Empathy. This is where problems arise and is exactly what we want to avoid at all costs.

_____

Empathy—the psychological identification with or vicarious experiencing of the feelings, thoughts, or attitudes of others.

_____

The truth is that if we really expect success, we must take into account how our plans and actions affect others. It's not enough that our actions have a tangible effect on others, it's also how others perceive you and your actions. People recognize when you display empathy, and it is then that they develop a positive emotional investment in your success because they know this success includes them.

If we're *Wired Differently* then we have to understand that this concept of *Empathy-Ego Balance* is a game changer. If you act solely upon *Empathy* without vision, discipline, and drive, you will likely flounder. Conversely, acting solely upon *Ego* without regard for others will mean that you'll lose your audience, that your team will not develop an emotional stake in the outcome because they perceive what's happening is all about you, not them.

So how then do we develop this *Empathy-Ego Balance*? Let me give you these five steps:

1. *When you make an entrance, be noticed appreciatively.* Be commanding. Be confident. Make yourself appear worthy of being in charge. At the same time, let others know that your efforts are about them. Your success is their success.

2. *Spend as much time on them as you have on yourself.* As you make plans, include others. Take into account not only how your

actions affect them, but also how they perceive you and the outcomes of your plans.

3. *Empathy, empathy, empathy.* Throughout your tenure as a leader, let others know that your efforts are on their behalf and you are attempting to understand their side.

4. *Have knowledge and command of the solution.* Nothing will make empathy evaporate like incompetence. Your people expect you to do your homework and negotiate on their behalf from a position of expertise. You can't know everything but that shouldn't prevent you from taking the counsel of experts. However, circumstances are not always cut-and-dried. We can't make decisions from fixed templates because variables always change. Effective leadership demands that we be resolute yet nimble, steadfast yet flexible. Your people need to know that the inevitable compromises were made for the best possible outcomes with them in mind.

5. *When you exit, be grateful.* When it's time to move on, let your people know that it was your privilege to interact with and serve them. Explain how others inspired you and even made you a better person.

Being *Wired Differently* means we recognize that our desires—and more crucially, our actions toward this important *Empathy-Ego Balance*—start with the *Fulcrum* of the *Mind*. We know that everything about who we are as individuals begins with the *Mind*. We are the sum of what we think and what actions we pursue.

To achieve success, we have to condition our minds to take those actions that move us in the right direction and avoid the *DriftAgain*. We must adopt the attitude of champion athletes and drill constantly, toughen our bodies, and discipline our thinking so that our reaction to any given situation is automatic. We condition ourselves by doing the "reps." This act of doing the reps rewires our thinking.

The process of rewiring your thinking is a fundamentally selfish exercise because you're focused inwardly on the *Ego*. What you're doing is training yourself to ignore the negatives about your situation and focus on the positive. In other words, remaining *Supremely Purposeful*.

Let's take it a step beyond that. To best take care of yourself you need a strong sense of self-esteem. This gives you confidence in your abilities and the momentum to get past the red lights that block your way forward.

What is counterintuitive about acting on the *Ego* is that its selfishness is what helps you recognize the *DriftAgain*, the phenomenon in which we allow ourselves to accept one compromise after another until we find ourselves far from where we should be. This acceptance of our circumstance is our *Land of Quo*.

To move forward involves change and we must embrace change because it is a constant of life. Even if we choose to do nothing, the world around us changes and before we know it, we've Drifted Again and are again stuck in that damn *Land of Quo*. To fight the *DriftAgain* we must take action and direct change toward purpose and success.

Not wanting to buck the system or constantly seeking the approval of others blinds us to the fact that we're stuck in the *Land of*

Quo. Acting on our *Ego* gives us a sense of awareness and that we need to keep ourselves first in our priorities.

If you're a parent, you have a lot of responsibilities keeping the family together and you have to best position yourself to provide for them. As your family circumstances change, you must accommodate them. Mentally, being the first at putting on your oxygen mask is not narcissism but key to survival.

If you're a business owner, the success of the company depends on you making the right decisions and to do so, you have to be selfish in how you apply yourself. And in the business world, you need no reminders to warn that if you stand still—in other words, get comfortable in your *Land of Quo*—you will get run over. To succeed in business and in life requires that you constantly rewire your thinking to adapt to the changing environment.

To rewire your thinking and develop the necessary confidence you must learn to respect your talents, abilities, and advantages— your *Favors.* And if you don't respect and love yourself, how can you expect others to do so?

———

"Nothing resembles selfishness more closely than self-respect."
-George Sand

———

However, don't get me wrong. If we become too focused on our *Ego*, then those traits can become counterproductive. We must learn to temper *Ego* with humility. Yes, we want to succeed. Yes, we want to push when others want to sit still. But we know we don't have all the answers, that we can make mistakes, and that we must listen to others.

Ironically, while those who act on their *Ego* are vilified as lacking in empathy, they are well aware of how people react to them. Ego-driven individuals pay attention to their appearance and strive to present a professional image. Working hand in hand with this awareness is that such people gravitate to those kinds of jobs where appearance, high expectations, and their elevated self-confidence prompt them to seek the top positions.

The Ego-driven have a drive to succeed and often act on a higher purpose. These individuals rise to become leaders because they see this higher purpose behind their actions, which is, they want to take care of others, the *Empathy-Ego Balance*. So, the act of being self-aware means that you're acting on behalf of the greater good for those around you. Hardly in keeping with what we've come to expect from the Ego-driven!

A leader aware of *Empathy-Ego Balance* can shine like a beacon to others, inspiring them to become aware of their own potential and, equally important, to take action to rewire their Minds and lead them out of their *Land of Quo*.

***

Let me give you a great example of when I learned the value of being Ego-driven.

The year was 1991. I was 26 and restarting my life after I'd dug myself into a deep hole, teetering on bankruptcy from my miserable losses in the donut business. I had a lot weighing on me: my financial future and my family as I had two infants to provide for. I was in the process of recreating myself and frankly, a bit unsure about my prospects. I needed to rebound but didn't know how to go about cultivating the attitude that I needed.

I knew that confidence, vanity, and even elements of narcissism were very powerfully engaging and comforting to possess and something I wanted in my own special and humble way. But frankly, I had a lot of failures under my belt and my self-esteem had taken a beating. I was stuck in my *Land of Quo* and to move forward, I needed to adopt the mindset of a champion.

My accomplishments and swagger as a collegiate athlete had since faded. I was searching for career success and recognition that had so far escaped me. Then I ran into an interesting man on the basketball court who turned my head around by knocking me on my ass!

He and I played pickup games at the same gymnasium and we ended up facing off on the court. For anyone critiquing our game, it was obvious we were not accomplished basketball players; junior-varsity bench warmers displayed more finesse than we did.

Not that it mattered. As we were full-contact guys, we engaged in a rough and tumble game. Whenever we stepped onto the court, we made certain to go after each other head-to-head.

Going against him elevated my performance. However, he continued to best me with his aggressive playing. He never let up. If a ball got loose, he and I ended up scrambling after it and fighting for possession.

It was us two crashing into the boards. We didn't stop until the game was over, and if we could, we'd jump into the next game, neither one of us wanting to let the other go unchallenged.

I had no idea who this guy was, his name, or what he did for a living. I just knew he was a fighter and a serious competitor who unknowingly demonstrated his core beliefs of focused determination and giving it all whenever he played.

The day finally came when we had the opportunity to talk. We were both walking out of the gym when I introduced myself and asked his name.

"Dean," he answered. "Doctor Dean."

I asked, "What kind of a doctor?"

What he then said became one of the most compelling things I've ever heard in my life. "I'm a heart doctor, the number-one cardiac surgeon in the Midwest." Without missing a beat, he added, "Actually, could be the best in the nation."

His answer floored me with its unabashed arrogance, and I loved him for it.

Worst-case scenario, if I ever needed heart surgery and I was close to flatlining, this Dr. Dean would be my number-one choice because he would fight and do what it took to resuscitate me.

In his day-to-day living, he wasn't going to tamp down his arrogance for the sake of being liked. That arrogance was an expression of his confidence and given his profession, it provided me with a deep sense of comfort should I ever have to call upon his services. And obliquely, this arrogance was an expression of *Empathy* because the doctor knew that if you needed heart surgery, then you wanted him.

What that incident taught me was that we have within us the potential and ability to lift ourselves and those around us with the correct cocktail of Empathy-Ego Balance in any situation. We are

Wired Differently to not only survive but to want others to come to us for what we have to offer. To be an expert in our field and be recognized as a leader with *Empathy-Ego Balance* means that we are driven to share our favors and gifts.

When faced with a crisis, what part of *Empathy-Ego Balance* would you turn to? Who's your Dr. Dean?

Are you anyone's Dr. Dean?

Is this what makes up your EGO?

E—Empathy, *for others.*

G—Go get it.

O—Others matter more.

———

"I can't actually have a big ego, because I've admitted I have one."
-Todd Saylor

———

CHAPTER FOUR

THE VIEW

"We clearly don't know, what we don't know,
*until we open our view." -***Todd Saylor**

It's strange how things are viewed through the lens of one person, how these things begin and how they end, and how they really exist versus the way they seem. In the culture of *Wired Different-ly*, this "View" manifests itself in how our *Wired Differently* traits shape and color the way we perceive the world and prompts us to move out of our *Land of Quo*.

My wife Traci and I were 30 years old when we found ourselves struggling to recover from career setbacks. We'd returned to Angola after my disastrous business experience earlier. We had lost a lot financially and thought it best that we move and start over. With that in mind, I decided on a plot of acreage in the woods east of Angola, Indiana.

The acreage was off a dirt road—a weedy, overgrown lot upon which sat a weather-beaten single-wide trailer in need of TLC. The remains of a half-assed garage leaned against the trailer. The structures were home to a colony of raccoons and surrounded by mounds of buried trash.

Across from the trailer stood a rusting 4,000-square-foot barn made of tin that was once the manufacturing start-up for a disposable lock company, since abandoned, then converted by a wandering wrench turner into an auto repair shop. Evidence of the mechanic's lack of trade craft was the black soot coating the barn's ceiling and walls from various car fires.

In between the trailer and the barn sat three manmade ponds. The reason for the ponds mystified me until I dredged their bottoms and hauled out the remains of a bizarre contraption that turned out to be a homemade submarine. This would-be Captain Nemo had been obviously testing his submersible in the ponds, no doubt when he wasn't busy burning up his barn.

The property was in such bad shape that I invited my insurance agent for a visit before I made a final inspection. When I asked, "What do you think this property deserves?" he calmly reached into his pocket and handed over a box of matches.

He returned to his car, shaking his head dismissively, and settled into the driver's seat, muttering, "If something unfortunate happens, I didn't see a thing." As he drove off, I remained there with the box of Blue Tip matches, wondering to myself, why is it that he saw only thirteen acres of ruin and waste, while all I saw were possibilities? A lot of hard work on my part to get there, for sure, but this place could be transformed into an amazing home for my young family. In my *View*, I saw a beautiful house, complete with a room that I would use as the headquarters for my future success. What was it about me that saw things so "Differently"? Did it spring from my desire to be *Supremely Purposeful*?

Although I had plenty of good intentions for the property, the reality was that all I had was five hundred dollars in our bank account. To develop these isolated acres, we'd have to tighten our belts, but the payoff would be an estate with beautiful landscaping, room for horses, and lots of space between us and the neighbors. It was my plan to build a magnificent home once I found my new business path and recovered financially.

While I made that happen, I figured why bother wasting money on rent? In the meantime, my family would live in a trailer that I owned, building equity on land upon which I would build a beautiful home to make for a wonderful living experience. Yep, I had big plans.

However, what I saw in my *View* differed from what the owner perceived. Other than the five hundred bucks cash, I had no money to buy the property. I wanted to convince him that the land was so undesirable that he should sell it to me for four thousand down on a five-year land contract balloon payment. Surely, I would recover in five years and by then, qualify for a loan.

Back and forth we went until he finally agreed, but I wasn't yet in the clear. I needed the four thousand cash for a down payment. I approached my bank, imploring them that I must have $3,500 to make this deal and that I'd make good on the loan.

The banker, Jerry Champion, was impressed by my earnestness. He smiled and said, "Let's try something 'differently.' Do you have any assets?"

I had to tell him the truth. "No."

"What did you drive here?"

"My two-year-old Ford Ranger that I use to deliver product in my sales job."

He said, "Bring me the auto loan info and the VIN."

When I returned, he looked over the documents, left, then came back into the office with a loan contract, asking me to sign, "Here. Here. And here."

"What's going on?" I asked.

He explained, "We now own the truck and here is your payment schedule." After I signed, he then handed over a $4,000 check and said, "Now go get your family's ranch."

Just like that, my *View* was clear, and I was on my way. In some respects, you could say that by acting *Wired Differently* and by being *Supremely Purposeful* I had allowed a miracle to happen. Jerry really trusted me as the truck wasn't worth four grand. I'm today forever grateful for his belief in me.

Eighteen months later my wife and I had done well enough that we bought a newer single-wide trailer to live in. The raccoons had for the most part been chased away. To work the land, we pinched pennies until we had enough saved to buy a 1950s vintage Ford 9N tractor. Though the tractor was manufactured before hydraulics were available, it managed to start most of the time and so was good enough for what we needed.

Late one afternoon I was on the tractor, getting ready to clear the acreage with a bush hog. That device is a heavy, five-foot-diameter mower towed behind the tractor that runs off its power drive.

My wife Traci and daughters Courtnee and Kendra, ages six and five, were outside watching me. I was happy and especially proud of my labors. I took a break to share with the family my vision for the land. I gestured where the horse fencing would go, where our house would stand, and how the landscaping would be developed someday. It was a fun time where we all saw the same glowing future. I loved it and hugged my daughters. Then it was back to work. I started the tractor and said to Traci, "Could you help me hook up this bush hog?"

Caught up in the moment, she eagerly jumped onto the tractor's driver's seat. Before I was ready, she engaged the lever to lower the device. Unfortunately, my hand was in the way, and it was caught beneath the edge of the bush hog. The mechanism's substantial weight caused it to settle into position, and lacking hydraulics, it could only be raised by being manhandled upward.

I was not only in a great deal of pain but terrified that my right hand was going to be horribly mangled. Traci could see me struggling but the weight of the bush hog was too much for her to lift. I didn't want her to get hurt helping me or have her risk leaving the kids alone if I had to go to the doctor.

She began to worry and cry. Our daughters picked up on her dread and they also began to cry in helpless fear at what was happening to Daddy.

Our closest neighbor was almost a half mile away, so urgent help was out of the question. Realizing there was no time to waste before I lost my hand, I calmly reassured Traci, "This situation was not your fault. Now take the girls behind the nearest tree and wait."

When they were hidden from view, I said a quick prayer for all to be okay, took three deep breaths, and yelled for power as I yanked my hand loose. Miraculously, my glove held together though my hand was a mess. My middle finger had been crushed flat as cardboard.

Cradling my injured hand, I kissed my wife and daughters, telling them I was going to be all right. I ran the quarter mile to our car and drove to the emergency room. A nurse led me to a separate examination room. The only treatment she offered was that I soak my gloved hand in saltwater while we waited for the doctor. Although still in extreme pain, I was optimistic that the doctor would arrive shortly and save my hand.

Ten minutes passed.

Then twenty.

A half hour. Forty-five minutes.

An hour.

An hour plus!

What was going on? My pain fueled rage and frustration. Why was I being ignored? Unless I received treatment soon, I was going to lose my finger despite my efforts to save it. In my mind's eye, I would never be able to hold my babies the same way again.

I festered about how incompetent and uncaring the doctor and this hospital staff were. Moment by moment my thoughts grew darker and darker.

Finally, the doctor entered the room with the nurse in tow. Both wore somber, stoic faces. I looked at him and was about to press him about my treatment.

Before I got a word out, he calmly said, "I'm sorry this took so long but the other guy didn't make it."

The other guy didn't make it. That kept ringing through my mind.

The *View* snapped with a new perspective. Suddenly I saw my situation completely differently. My injured finger didn't seem so important considering the doctor was trying to save a dying man. And despite his best efforts, the doctor had come up short. Now he had to deal with me.

At that moment I was humbled and even shamed for my selfish take on the situation. The experience seared me with the realization that the *View* should be wide and encompassing.

True, we in the culture of *Wired Differently* must be focused on where we want to be and how to get there. After all, we need a strong vision to navigate out of our *Land of Quo*. But we can't allow our *View* to be so narrow that we don't see our place in the world.

So, my advice for when it seems that life is doing its worst to you: use my example and remind yourself, *the other guy didn't make it.*

"In all trials, the beauty becomes greater than the anguish."
-Napoleon Hill

***

The *View* illuminates a path forward but the "Wired Differently View" is full of ambition and risk. Why is *View* important? Because life has a way of dragging us down if we let it. It's too easy to be swamped by cynicism and negativity to the point that you don't see the blessings in your life, much less the opportunities.

View gives us perspective. Oftentimes, looking at a situation from a different angle will show you things that you'd missed. For example, one trick that artists use to critique their work is to study it through a mirror or to turn it upside down. This way, the mistakes in the work jump right out.

How do we establish a *Wired Differently View*?

- Be grateful. If you start from a position of gratitude, you won't be stewing over why things are so bad, quite the opposite. You'll be asking yourself *How can I make things better?* Put yourself in the right frame of mind, and you'll be surprised by what good news will come your way. Gratitude is the foundation of happiness. Too many people postpone happiness until they reach a particular goal. How many times have you heard a variation of this: *Once I make a million dollars, then I'll be happy.* Trust me, once you make a million dollars, life will continue to test you. Be happy now and do it through gratitude.
- Red lights are just that, *Red Lights*. They eventually turn green. When you hit a red light, take that as an opportunity to inventory your favors. Don't sweat the small stuff. Now I'm the first to emphasize that in any project, the devil is in the details. But don't dwell on petty annoyances or minor decisions and thus allow them to inflate into showstoppers.
- Everyone's got an opinion. Take advice from well-intentioned family and associates for what it's worth. In my anecdote earlier, the insurance agent thought he was doing me a favor with his grim appraisal of my property. Sure, I could understand his perspective; that was obvious. The land needed a lot of attention. Problem for him was that he wasn't

willing to factor in all the work I was committed to doing. For me, to turn that neglected plot of land into a choice parcel of real estate, I'd leverage two of my favors: *Distance* and *Execution*. When you look at a situation through your *View*, cycle through your favors and then determine what opportunities come into focus.

- Be more empathetic. Regardless of how much of a big shot you think you are, the world doesn't revolve around you. If you croak tonight, the sun will still rise tomorrow. It's easy to get so wrapped up in our personal drama that we fail to see how others are struggling through the same situation. This is a reason to make *View* a key component of your leadership palette, that you as a leader have to see beyond your immediate circumstances. In doing so, you will not succumb to *DriftAgain*. You'll see the bigger picture of what's going on and make the necessary adjustments to your plans and behaviors.

- This too shall pass. Nothing lasts forever. This applies to both the good and the bad that occur in our life. Cherish the good and savor those moments, using them as opportunities to make things better. When Lady Luck gives you snake eyes, then deal with it, use that setback to take stock of your situation—It's only a Red Light! Time to inventory your favors—then decide on a course of action and move forward.

- Our world exists on many planes. The physical plane is obvious—the weeds, the racoons, the dilapidated tin barn—but it's more than what our eyes see that matters just as much. What is a vision other than an idea in your head? Yet that idea, and the hope and faith that fuel its power, can be a mighty force. If we perceive only the negative, then we're stuck in a regressive state. But if our *View* is through the lens of positivity, we can see paths forward and because we're *Wired Differently*, we have no choice but to follow them.

- Use your *View* to remain *Supremely Purposeful.*

———

*"Some men see things as they are, and ask why. I dream of things that never were, and ask why not." -**Robert Kennedy***

———

***

Years later, I received an enlightened lesson on what the *View* means. I was on business, driving through one of my least favorite cities, Cleveland. (Sorry guys, but I gotta be honest.) And to make my visit worse, it was a sloppy, cold, rainy day. Absolutely miserable. To heap on that misery, I was in the dumps on account of a lousy sales day. Nothing was going the way I wanted it to. The need to pay bills was breathing down my neck and I was deeply stressed.

I needed a break. I needed a sale. I needed some good news.

The weather got even worse, and all that wet grayness pulled me further into this emotional downer.

I got so depressed that I wanted to cry. Me! Big, tough All-American football player, Mr. Never-say-die-always-look-at-the-positive master salesman. I was that unhappy.

Please God, I prayed, *give me something. Give me a nudge to show that I can go the distance. If you can hear me, please, prove that my prayers mean something. I'm not asking for much. Just part the clouds. Give me a sliver of sunshine to demonstrate that you hear me. Please God. Give me some hope to cling to.*

No sooner did I finish that prayer than the rain turned to hail. Torrents of hail roared upon me and pounded the car. The hail got so bad I thought people were going to get killed.

I glanced to the skies, dark and turbulent as an angry sea. *God, what's going on? You did the exact opposite!* I must have pissed Him off something majorly. *My dear Lord, I'm not sure what's going on.*

Now I felt even lower than before, worthless. God surely heard my cries for help, and He unleashed this storm to say He's turned His back on me. All I asked for was a little sunshine, a symbol of hope, and He wasn't even giving me that.

Lost and frustrated, and smothered by rain and hail, as I rounded the corner, a billboard started to appear in the stormy murk.

I turned on my headlights and in perfect cadence with the rhythm of the wipers, that billboard presented a gigantic image of a cartoon rising sun, a big smiling yellow face—an ad for the Sunshine Baking Company. There was the ray of sunshine I'd been praying for.

Right there, I let the car coast to a halt as I cried and thanked Him.

He answered:

You see, Todd, it's not always what you want.

You see, Todd, it's not always about your view.

You see, Todd, I'm in charge and I love you and I want you to start seeing things differently. Your view needs to be broader and less about your perspective but rather about Mine and others.

It's not always how we want things or want Him.

It's not always how we plan it or plan on Him.

It's not always what we expect or what we even deserve...but it's always in our *View*.

God shows that your works and distance are the mission we are doing on His behalf.

Then, where are you? Adjust your *View* every so often and be open to His possibilities.

Let's do this thing called life, *Wired Differently,* together. It'll depend on your VIEW.

V—Visualize the possibilities, then Look again, Differently.

I—Interpret what's happening, then re-interpret, Differently.

E—Extend the Game until you can see a path to Victory, Differently.

W—Willingness to receive help from others, and submit to a higher Power, God.

———

"It's not what you look at that matters, it's what you see."
-Henry David Thoreau

———

CHAPTER FIVE

THE PAIN

*"Going the Distance requires pain, but the reward is, you've Gone the Distance." -**Todd Saylor***

Let me show you how Wired Differently I am.

I thank God for my pain.

I say that because I know pain. Here are the different ways that I've felt pain as I list them in my W.D.R. (Wired Differently Résumé). I encourage you to create your own W.D.R. and reflect upon your own amazing feats to inspire and propel you through times. Don't hesitate to marvel at what you've overcome as you update your W.D.R.

So here I go:

Pain of feeling not being wanted,

Pain of feeling not good enough,

Pain of feeling trapped with no way out,

Pain of feeling no possibility of being loved.

The pain of a:

Broken back,

Two broken hands,

Ten dislocated fingers,

Three broken fingers,

Two broken ribs,

Two meniscus tears,

Broken collarbone,

Calcified femur muscle,

Morbid MRSA cellulitis,

Three ruptured discs in back,

Three back surgeries,

Severed foot,

Ten concussions,

Two broken bursa sacs,

Mangled face, a horse ripped my nose off my face,

Bald,

Reconstructive face surgery,

Three times broken nose,

Crushed finger,

Blow-out hernia,

Six head-on car collisions,

Frauded for over $300,00,

Embezzled out of over $250,000,

Parental divorce,

Marriage on brink,

Child miscarriage,

Lost everything twice,

Depressed,

Hated,

Criticized,

Judged,

Bullied,

Beaten up,

Burglarized,

Even jailed…

From this list you can see that I've suffered emotional pain and physical pain.

Which is worse?

Let me tell you, give me physical pain any day.

Why is that? Because what led to physical pain put me on the path that made me a better person. Suffering physical pain was the first step to recovery. Enduring that physical pain was part of a cathartic process that helped me overcome emotional pain.

Why should we welcome physical pain? Because it's a reminder that we're alive and that such pain is leading to something good.

For me, getting a wound stitched up was part of the lesson of what to do better next time.

Floor burns on my body were trophies of a hard-fought battle.

Forcing myself to run one more mile brought pride and confidence.

Lifting one more set of weights was the price of getting stronger.

Knee and back surgery were grueling ordeals but necessary to my health.

———

*"Scars have the strange ability to remind us that the past was real and we are successful." -****Cormac McCarthy***

———

To show how *Wired Differently* I've always been about pain, let me share these anecdotes from my childhood. As a boy, I would beg my six-year-old brother to play with me—sports mostly—and the only way I could get him to cooperate was if I let him belt me with a Hot Wheels track. Each smack of that length of plastic felt good because to me it was a marker that I was getting closer to what I wanted. Okay, sounds a little weird perhaps, but if you're *Wired Differently*, you understand. Later during the sixth grade, I'd made a rude gesture to a classmate; yes, *that* rude gesture. The teacher saw what I'd done and called me out on it. "Todd, at the end of the day you're going to see the principal for this."

With certain punishment looming over my head, plus the guilt of what I'd done, I decided to get past my anxiety. I raised my hand and asked permission to go to the restroom. Instead, I went straight to the principal and explained what I had done.

He gave me a quizzical look. "What do you want from me?"

"I did wrong and deserve a spanking." I looked at the paddles hanging on his wall. "Why do you have two boards, and one has holes?"

"The one with holes hurts more."

"I'll take that one."

The principal didn't question my motives. He simply grasped the board. "Okay, Todd, bend over."

Swat! Swat!

"Now return to class. I'll be checking with your father. Be sure to explain what just happened."

I straightened. "Yes, sir."

That was the end of it. No lengthy apologies from me. No lecture from him. No more guilt. I learned my lesson. I was simply a sixth grader making the connection between pain and gain. That night I slept soundly, untroubled by what I'd put myself through.

Now here I am, 55 years old and still drawing from that lesson of how physical pain led to repentance, then to redemption, and finally to absolution.

The Two Forms of Pain

Pain comes to you in two forms. Physical, the one that *Bleeds*. Emotional, the one that taps into your *Needs*.

And you can make both work for you.

We *Wired Differently* people crave physical pain for the muscle it builds, the lessons it imparts, and the subsequent healing that it brings. Without experiencing physical pain, we let ourselves stay average, we *DriftAgain*, we remain in the Land of Quo. We need pain to jar us out of complacency and remind us that we have work to do.

Let's use weight training as a metaphor. If we want to get stronger, we lift weights to the moment of pain or failure.

It's at this point that the muscle breaks down and the cellular fibers get ripped apart. The body then repairs the damaged tissue with protein, filling and growing the cells larger than they were before. This of course takes time. Growth and improved strength take place during this healing phase of the cell. It's not the lifting of weights that builds big muscles but the recovery that occurs from the healing cells. The physical pain we experience during this entire process occurs when we lift weights to failure and then the ache and soreness that accompany the recovery. All this pain lets us know we've pushed our body into a state of growth.

That's the understanding of the *Bleeds*.

The *Needs* is quite a bit different.

While we humans like to regard ourselves as an enlightened species, we are at our core, emotional creatures. Even what we consider as our most logical, thoughtful decisions are but rationalizations of an emotional response to a stimulus.

Given that we are emotional creatures, then if emotional pain becomes too uncomfortable, we tend to retreat from it since these *Needs* are tougher to manage than the *Bleeds*. Emotional pain can overwhelm our ability to cope, becoming debilitating and catastrophic to our well-being.

We might want to dismiss *Needs* pain as being simply "all in your head," but emotional pain is quite real. Failing to address it can lead to detrimental consequences and here's why:

Emotional Pain endures

If you've ever broken a bone or suffered an injury that left scars, think back to the incident. What comes to mind is not the physical pain but the emotional sensations that you had at the time. Recall an episode of intense physical pain. We remember that whatever caused the pain brought a lot of hurt. However, we don't relive the physical pain; the emotions around what happened rush back to us, as vivid and distressing as when that *Bleeds* pain was first inflicted.

To illustrate this, if your knee is torn during a football game, you hurry to recover as fast as possible and get back onto the field. If you end up playing in the same stadium where you were injured, so much the better as you'll reclaim that space as your triumph over a setback.

Needs pain is quite different. Now recall an uncomfortable situation: a romantic breakup; the loss of a job; bad news about a close relative. The emotional pain will rush back at you, sometimes almost as strong as when you first experienced it. After a breakup, you'll steer clear of your favorite hangouts with the ex. If anyone asks why, you'll have a ready answer: Because the memory of those places is too painful.

So, a broken heart is more painful than a broken leg!

We get more empathy from Physical Pain

If you've had a broken arm or leg, didn't you invite others to sign your cast? Or if you were sewn up, unbutton your shirt to show the stitches? How did the others react? No doubt, with curiosity and empathy.

But what about those times when you suffered emotional trauma? The loss of a loved one, a divorce, a career setback. Chances are that only your closest associates might want to talk about your troubles, or you might get a sympathy card, but that's the extent of the empathy. You might even have been told, "Go to therapy and keep it to yourself." Some even avoid you because of the uncertainty of knowing how to act.

We're more proactive about Physical Pain.

If you're like most normal Americans, you probably have a first aid kit handy. We're more ready to deal with cuts, sprains, and bruises than we are with rejection and failure. We know how to clean a wound and apply a bandage. But tell us bad news and we're at a loss. How do we cope? Some of us have training in helping others with emotional pain, but when it happens to us, then we are lost and thrashing for answers and a way out of the despair.

We'll take therapy classes to treat shoulder surgery, but classes to mend a broken heart can become too personal and uncomfortable. The irony is, to truly help another person with their emotional pain we must build empathy, and that empathy can in turn provoke strong, uncomfortable emotional reactions within us. This is why grief counselors burn out so readily.

Emotional Pain can do more damage than Physical Pain to our spiritual and mental health.

Let's briefly return to your school days. You are certainly painfully aware of every failing grade that you received. They filled you with a fear of failure and the dread of not being good enough. If you were in a fistfight, you've no doubt forgotten the pain from the injuries, if not the fight itself. But I'm sure you remember the emotions that led to the fight. Anger. Fear. Frustration. Feeling trapped.

Such lingering emotional scars are why bullying is so traumatic. It's not the actual physical pain the bully inflicted, but the anxiety and their use of intimidation to control you. Your self-esteem suffers. The humiliation leaves deep emotional scars that may never heal. Even recalling experiences of being bullied can bring back panic attacks and bouts of depression.

Emotional Pain is physically real.

Until now I've been discussing the difference between *Bleeds* pain and *Needs* pain, and at this point I have to mention the overlap between the two. Physiologically, where do we experience pain? For example, if we mash our fingers, the pain receptors in our fingers transmit the pain signal through our nerves to our brain. For us to feel the pain, the brain must register the sensation. However, we do not feel the pain in our brain but in whatever part of the body experienced the injury.

So then, if we've been rejected by a loved one, why do we say that we've got a broken heart? Because that's how our body internalizes such intense emotion. Strong feelings of excitement, desire, and belonging invoke hormonal and cardiovascular changes. Our chest tightens. Our pulse and heart rate increase. Then upon rejection and loss, those same physical reactions come back into play.

These are not the only physical reactions to emotional responses. When we get angry, we see red from the blood rushing to our face. Bad news can make a delicious meal taste instantly sour. It's not uncommon to hear information so unsettling that we throw up.

The big difference between *Needs* pain and *Bleeds* pain is that emotional pain carves a deep wound into our psyche. Because of this, we're reluctant to willingly move toward anything that provokes *Needs* pain.

But we do have a secret weapon. *Bleeds* pain is a great way to alleviate *Needs* pain. This is why physicians and therapists recommend regular, vigorous exercise during times of stress and anxiety. The act of immersing ourselves in physical activity helps our brain cope with emotional pain.

***

It's imperative that we learn to handle emotional pain the same way we handle physical pain. Because since we're *Wired Differently*, and serious about staying out of our Land of Quo, then we must correct for our *DriftAgain* and make the necessary if uncomfortable decisions and follow through with decisive action.

We must commit ourselves to go the Distance. And going the Distance is never easy. It involves *Bleeds* pain and *Needs* pain. What causes us to go the Distance is our response to *Needs* pain. We have to admit to some uncomfortable truths about ourselves—the *Needs* pain—and that we're not happy in our Land of Quo. Going the Distance will involve *Bleeds* pain at some point. To grasp what is currently out of reach, we must stretch our muscles and our minds.

As we've already established the link between *Bleeds* and *Needs* pain, then to offset the emotional pain, we subject ourselves to physical pain, or at least discomfort. As we're *Wired Differently*, we know to succeed we must inventory our favors and remain *Supremely Purposeful*.

To begin, let's discuss the fulcrum of the Mind. We know that everything starts with the mind. From *Wired Differently*:

"How your mind conceptualizes the world and reacts to events determines your behavior. In other words, how your mind works affects how you will act, and how you act shapes how you will live."

We condition ourselves to perform actions that require that we rewire our mind into productive routines. We acknowledge our hesitation at moving from comfort to discomfort as a *Needs* pain, an emotional obstacle that we must overcome.

Furthermore, we acknowledge that we are an Elite and deserve to be treated as such. Conversely, as Elites, then we must behave accordingly. Elites don't shy from their challenges or go easy on themselves.

What we can't do is avoid *Needs* pain by displacing the pain with unhealthy habits and self-defeating behavior. To blunt the anxiety of emotional pain, people procrastinate. Or too often, they resort to alcohol and drugs. However, healthy outlets like working out, socializing, meditation, or prayer allow us to redirect our emotional energy and ease the worry and heartache.

Without pain we can't move out of our Land of Quo. To overcome our *Bleeds* and *Needs* pain, we shouldn't hesitate to call upon our Maker for guidance.

We discussed in *Wired Differently* our big motivators, the three P's:

Pride,

Power,

Plenty.

Now consider that Plenty is actually the opposite of *Needs* pain. When you have plenty, then you don't have emotional pain.

The Bible explains that it's easier for a camel to go through the eye of a needle than it is for a rich man to inherit the Kingdom. What's that all about? To begin, it's clear the rich man has no emotional pain. As such, he has no need to heal. Or stretch. Or learn. There is no reason to ask for help from a higher power. A rich man is perfectly content in his Land of Quo. He will never change. Free of *Needs* pain, there is nothing to motivate him to correct his *Drift*. With no reason for him to seek God, he therefore never thinks about reaching the Kingdom.

To go the Distance, to live as *Wired Differently*, we should not avoid pain. Rather, we embrace pain for the lessons, the growth, and the strength that it will bring.

Let's think of PAIN using this acronym:

P—Power...Pain gives us power and confidence once overcome.

A—Accept...Pain *Needs* accepted, not avoided, nor run from.

I—Integral...Pain is the epoxy bond that sturdies our being and internal fortitude.

N—Need...We need Pain to guide us and grow us and to protect us.

———

"Every adversity comes with equal or greater benefit."
-Napoleon Hill

———

CHAPTER SIX

THE ODD

*"Our oddities define us as uniquely Wired Differently. We need The
Odd to clearly separate us from being average." -**Todd Saylor***

Odd? Who wants to be *Odd?* When you call someone an *oddball,*
you're not doing them any favors. No one wants to be the *odd man
out.* We are socialized to fit in. That's what peer pressure is all
about.

Let's look at the *"Differently"* part of being in the culture of
Wired Differently. Being different, by definition, means not being
the same as others, it means sticking out, it means being *Odd.*

We as individuals are the combined result of both our environment and what's been passed down genetically from our parents. Just as we've inherited the color and shape of our eyes, so too
have we inherited many of our mannerisms and traits. My dad was
definitely an odd sort, and his personal traits and unconventional
methods certainly contributed to his success as a football coach.
From early on my dad recognized that I, like him, was *Wired Differently* and he used that to trick me in his fatherly way and to get
me to do those crazy kinds of stunts that are the hallmark of being
Wired Differently Todd.

———

*"Do not conform to the pattern of this world." -**Romans 12:2***

———

***

It was the summer of 1977. I was 12 and working in the family donut shop at the Lake James resort near Angola, Indiana. My shift was over and I called my dad for a ride home. I was using the shop's kitchen phone, one of those vintage wall models with a long cord. Right after I asked him for the ride, my dad mentioned that I should run home to beat his record.

Without hesitation, I replied, "What's the record? Start the clock." I dropped the phone and sprinted out the door, determined to beat my dad's record. Our summer work cottage was a mile away and it was the middle of a hot and humid Indiana afternoon.

In retrospect, as I dashed home, I couldn't recall if my father had ever mentioned running the route, how long the route actually was, or even the time it had him taken to do so. I had no idea of what the record was, or if one even existed. When I got home, I raced to the end of the fishing pier, where my dad sat, drinking a Coke. Breathlessly, I asked him about the record. He glanced at his watch, then remarked, "Eight minutes, thirty seconds. Just missed it."

When I grew older and began to understand my dad's thinking, I drew two lessons from this experience. One—my dad knew how to motivate me. And two—that he had settled in for the day and didn't want to pick me up from the shop.

So what does it mean to be *Odd?* First of all, it does not mean being wacky or weird for the sake of being wacky or weird. And it goes beyond just having a few quirks. Being *Odd* means daring to be different by leveraging your *Favors* to get out of your *Land of Quo.*

If we want to separate ourselves from the pack, we have to be different. In a foot race, the difference is obvious; you're the one running faster. But if we dig into this example, we have to ask, what allowed you to run faster? The answer would be your attitude, the way you harnessed your drive—your willingness to go the *Distance,* your willingness to *Attack,* your willingness to exploit your *Edge,* all of which manifested themselves in your training long before you began the race.

Study anyone who achieved success in their proven field, you will see that they did something different and were in fact frequently dismissed as quite *Odd.*

Look at Gandhi. At the start of his struggle for the independence of India, he dressed the part of an educated lawyer to express his refinement and respectability. Soon he realized that the British would never acknowledge that he was anything more than an ungrateful, dark-skinned upstart. So rather than try to ingratiate himself into their way of thinking, he did the opposite. He rejected western clothing and dressed only in the simple garb that we've come to know him by. What the world saw was this humbly attired champion of the downtrodden standing up to the mighty British Empire. By European standards, Gandhi was definitely regarded as *Odd,* and he leveraged that difference as his strength.

And in your profession, what are you doing to stand out? What keeps you from acting upon what makes you *Odd*? Do you keep quiet at meetings because you fear that your ideas will be dismissed as crazy?

Being *Odd* is getting over the reluctance to say only what we think others want to hear and to do only what we think others want us to do. Being labeled *Odd* is used against us. We are browbeaten to conform. We fall victim to the "tall poppy syndrome." Stand too tall and get your head cut off. Better to hide in the crowd.

But progress in any endeavor can only happen by doing something new. Since we're venturing into new territory, expect plenty of false starts. You will only know if an idea is good or bad when you try it. This willingness to take chances is a trait of being *Wired Differently*.

Here is how Scott Adams, the eccentric, cartoonist genius behind *Dilbert*, achieved success:

―――

"Scott Adams has…built his successful career mainly through trial and error—a whole lot of error, to be exact."
-Harvard Business Review

―――

Too often, we measure success in terms of popularity. But remember that things—songs, politicians, fashion, opinions—are popular because they sit so comfortably within the *Land of Quo*.

In growing up, we're trained to accept the status quo, in other words, to take up residence in the *Land of Quo*. But if we're *Wired*

Differently, we recognize the trap. In accepting compromise after compromise, we've allowed ourselves to *DriftAgain*. As we realize that we're not living up to our potential, not being *Supremely Purposeful*, and letting opportunity slip through our fingers, frustration sets in.

But when you embrace the *Odd*, you're aware of your authentic self and will acknowledge that what makes you *Odd* are your strengths.

Being *Odd* isn't easy. Take for example, these two "Oddities" who changed the world. We have to admit that being *Odd* is choosing the harder path. Sometimes it might mean being unlikeable and even downright prickly. Steve Jobs was known for not caring if he rubbed you the wrong way. When he was hired as a teenager by HP, his manager had the foresight to assign Jobs to the night shift where he was less likely to cause trouble. As luck would have it, it was there where he befriended Steve Wozniak—an electronics nerd known for his pranks and unorthodox ideas—and the two partnered in several ventures that eventually led to Apple Computers. Jobs was a perfectionist, and it was that attention to detail that made Apple products stand out from the competition. He was a man with big ideas and strong opinions and wasn't interested in being popular. Steve Jobs embraced the *Odd*. Ironically, it was his success as a visionary and innovator that made him popular.

If you're *Wired Differently*, then how do you succeed at being *Odd*? Here's how:

- Inventory your *Favors*.
- Be a role model. Set the example.
- Set high standards for yourself and live up to them.

- Follow through—go the *Distance*. You must finish what you start.
- Recognize that you can *DriftAgain*.
- Do whatever it takes to get out of your *Land of Quo*.

Let's backtrack a bit to discuss something that's scientifically orthodox but not considered *Odd*. Even as we're *Wired Differently* from an attitudinal standpoint, if we start by looking at the development of the human brain, we can see that every one of us develops our thinking through a similar and amazingly phenomenal process.

Before you're born, and when you're inside your mom's belly, you're developing as many as 250,000 neurons every minute. Neurons are the cells in your brain, spinal column, and nerves that conduct impulses throughout your body. When you enter this world, your brain will have more than 100 billion neurons. After you're born, your brain continues to grow and by the time you're six, you will possess a staggering 1,000 trillion neurons.

Even though I graduated with a business degree from Manchester University—what I consider the best accounting school in the country—and understand numbers, I had to look up how many zeros a trillion represents, only to find out that 1,000 trillion isn't even a number; it's actually called a quadrillion. It's such an immense number that if you started counting at the age of two, by the time you reached a quadrillion you would've lived and died over 45,000 lifetimes. Literally, I've done the math.

In your mother's womb, your neurons develop unconnected from each other. At the instant you are born, think of your mind as a blank slate. The reason why children from the ages of three to ten can learn so fast is because of the disproportionate number of neurons that are waiting to be connected during this period of intense brain activity. When we get around the age of 12, the neurons which are not used are lost through a pruning process so that the brain can improve the connections already made. This is why our job as parents is so important. We must push our children to learn the skills and habits we want them to have. As these neurons connect, they are covered by a sheath of myelin tissue that shields the connections and allows the nerve cells to work much more efficiently.

As you experience events, your brain learns and builds memory. It detects patterns. It learns cause and effect. Because of the myelin sheath growing over the neuron connections, your brain physically gets *wired*.

Neuroplasticity is the idea that through the subconscious, we can conform and mold our brains to think the way we want to. We actually have the capability to *rewire our minds!* As adults we must understand that if we're not who we want to be, we can become who we want to be. If there is something we want, we can get it. But we don't know how to get those things unless we've mastered this great ability of the neuroplasticity of our brain, to be shaped and re-conformed into thinking the way we need to be thinking to get what we want.

As you can imagine, quadrillion neurons represent a significant amount of brain power, but to fully exploit all that thinking potential, you must act upon the unique cultural traits that make you *Wired Differently*. Life has a way of pulling us into the *Land of Quo*, to accept the routine compromises that can ensnare us in a net that even those quadrillion neurons are powerless to liberate us from, unless we act upon what makes us *Odd*.

———

*"As the twig is bent, so grows the tree." -**Alexander Pope***

———

Our wiring forms during childhood and we develop traits and habits that define who we are. However, we know that we can re-wire our thinking. To undertake this, we first acknowledge that we are *Wired Differently*, that we have to fight against the *DriftAgain* and to do so, we inventory our *Favors* and leverage them to move out of our *Land of Quo*. What motivates us to become high achievers is that we're culturally *Odd*, that we embrace what it takes to be *Supremely Purposeful*.

This desire to be special starts when we are toddlers. We want both affirmation and approval. How many of us remember these pleas from childhood?

"Daddy, look at me."

"Daddy, I'll be good."

"Daddy, I'll never leave you."

"Daddy, don't leave me."

While I mentioned that being *Odd* is to separate ourselves from the pack, even if it means not being popular, on the other hand *Wired Differently* people can't help craving approval if that's what it means to win.

***

Here's a great example of me embracing the *Odd* to win approval and grasp success.

I was on a sales tour visiting clients in Columbus, Ohio, with Jimmy Lenhart riding shotgun. If you remember from my first book, *Wired Differently*, when Jim and I met, he had just left the insurance industry and was selling cleaning chemicals.

Two years prior to this trip, when I switched to the PEO industry, he jumped at the chance to join my fledgling sales team. I couldn't have picked a better partner. Jim was about twenty years older than me and had cut his teeth on the insurance business. He was a seasoned salesman with a clever, forceful style. Physically, he was a balding 50-year-old, wore big glasses, and was in primo shape. He had the ability to cut you down with a piercing look, then put you in stitches with his smile and easy humor.

Jim and I had perfected the Power Spin Sale, which is to find all the pain a client has before we begin our sales presentation. In a Spin Sale, once the client's pain has been flushed out in previous calls, we would organize our solutions around their needs. I added Power to the Spin Sale formula because this technique worked best when we got the client to actually provide the solution to their own sales problems.

Jim and I were now collaborating on sales calls. His forte was his dry humor and his expertise in health insurance. Mine was my command of the overall sale and sales strategy. We took each sales opportunity seriously and learned what the client needed, what their pain was, and worked every angle to present our proposals.

During our first calls together, we had fun playing "good cop, bad cop" during our client pitches. In spite of his good humor, Jim was all too eager to play bad cop...and then take it too far. He was also willing to do odd things at my expense.

There was this time when I was going over my credit card statement with my assistant Stacy when she noted that the previous month, I had spent $3,000 in Las Vegas.

That puzzled me and I said, "I wasn't in Vegas last month."

Stacy rolled her eyes. Then I remembered that the expenses had been charged around Jim's fiftieth birthday. His office was two doors down the hall, and I yelled in his direction, "Jimmy, were you in Vegas last month?"

He answered, "Yes, I was."

I glanced at the statement. "Did you skydive?"

"Yes, I did."

"Did you take my card?"

"Yes, I did."

"Were you using it?"

"Yes, I did."

His answer perplexed me. I pressed, "Why should I pay for this?"

"You have tons of money and it was on my bucket list."

I had to laugh. That answer got him off the hook.

Back to the sales call. We were on our last stop before heading home, an auto sales auction company. We'd visited them four times already and our patience was running thin. During negotiations they'd want us to buy them lunch, and when we reached the time to either close the deal or cut and run, they'd drag their feet and put off their decision for yet another meeting.

This time we didn't take the client to lunch and pitched them in their office. But as before, they demurred and wouldn't commit to a decision. Both Jim and I were done with their stalling. I was considering a "Blow the Deal to Make the Deal" type of attack to close. That's certainly a *Wired Differently* sales move, basically the "Hail Mary" of sales pitches when you're at your wit's end and are willing to "Blow the Deal to Make the Deal." This is a certain move that allows us as the sales team to take control of the decision process. What we're telling the customer is that if you say no to these terms, if and when we ever come back, the deal won't ever be as good.

I again reviewed the financial wins, the final benefits and features, and was about to start my "Blow the Deal" move when Jim, on cue, launched into his bad-cop rant, then he stared at me and said, "Todd, you've done everything possible to make this deal except stand on your head."

Then Jim's eyes widened and he grinned, signaling, *Oh crap! What did I just say to Todd?*

Without hesitation, I dropped to the floor and rolled into a pike-position head stand as I interrupted Jim to complete the presentation. Upside down, I recited the closing marks, declaring that I'd go the distance and even stand on my head if that meant keeping Jim from talking. He remained in character, as I did, and we won that client's mind and heart.

Sadly, I must admit, Jim has since passed away and I miss him.

***

Wired Differently people are odd and we must embrace the *Odd*. This willingness to separate and distinguish ourselves from others is a cultural trait that helps us fight the *DriftAgain* and get out of our *Land of Quo*.

Remember what it means to be:

O—Outlandish, going beyond what is expected.

D—Differently, we do things Differently, an adverb that modifies an adjective:

to break out of the Status Quo.

D—Distance, "It's not just the efforts that we make,

but more the distance we will go."

———

"Why blend in when you can stand out?" -**Dr. Seuss**

———

CHAPTER SEVEN

NO MAS MOMENT!

*"Recognize when your No Mas Moment is upon you,
before it is on you." -**Todd Saylor***

Wired Differently people are fighters. Wired Differently people go the distance. But Wired Differently people must also have the wherewithal to say *No Mas! No More!*

How can this be? Isn't the idea of *No Mas* contradictory to everything about being *Wired Differently*?

Not at all. This came to me as an epiphany when watching a documentary about Roberto Durán, a professional boxer from Panama whose nickname was "Hands of Stone." On June 20, 1980, he faced Sugar Ray Leonard, himself an Olympic gold medalist and professional world champion. Durán won by unanimous decision.

Sugar Ray didn't like losing and with his eyes set on settling the score, he continued to train hard. For his part, Durán, having grown up dirt poor, found himself showered with money and adulation. He partied 'round the clock, drinking heavily, and ballooned in weight. Certain that Durán would let himself go, Sugar Ray lobbied for a second fight to take place before the end of the year. He knew Durán would be financially pressured to accept the fight and try to "sweat it out" to bring his weight down to the required 147 pounds.

The fight took place on November 25, 1980, in the New Orleans, Louisiana Superdome. During the bout, Sugar Ray danced around Durán, stinging him with well-timed punches. As the fight progressed, Sugar Ray applied psychological warfare against Durán, taunting him, jabbing and then stopping to mug with his chin out, daring Durán to come after him.

Durán was not only in poor fighting shape; he was also in great discomfort, having taken diuretics and laxatives when he crash-dieted to lose weight. Stomach cramps weakened him, and he was most likely in danger of crapping his pants in front of the whole world. Realizing that he had let himself get humiliated by Sugar Ray and was the victim of his own demise, Durán had nothing to gain in continuing the fight any longer. In the eighth round, Durán turned to the referee and said, *"No mas."* No more. The bout was awarded to Sugar Ray in a technical knockout.

Did Durán quit? As I watched the fight, I realized that he was me and those other people who have found themselves in scenarios where we don't want to quit, where we don't have *quit* in us. In fact, we don't even understand what that means. But like Durán, we might find ourselves in situations where we have a bad choice and a worse choice. When that happens, we must acknowledge that we can change our vernacular and instead of saying "I quit," we say, "No More." *No Mas!*

Consider it a readjustment in our life so we can survive to fight another day. The Wired Differently person wants to go on, needs to go on. Without hesitation, they will go the distance because they're wired that way. Unfortunately, this can become a component of *DriftAgain*.

How so?

We need to understand that if we go on, we'll do harm to ourselves, and so we have to give ourselves permission to say *No Mas*. If we don't, and we take it too far, then we're bringing collateral damage not just on ourselves, but on our families and our tribes. When we let that happen, we're not making the right decisions as leaders. We can't crap our pants on world TV in front of our family. We *Wired Differently* people must have this conversation with ourselves or we will definitely crap our pants, and often. We must confront this fundamental *DriftAgain* characteristic, openly and loudly.

Going back to Roberto Durán…what happened to him? After the fight, he was thoroughly vilified in his home country of Panama. But he recaptured his health and trained hard for a third bout against Sugar Ray, which Durán lost in a decision. He continued to fight professionally until retiring in 2001. Afterwards he had parts in cinema and television and embarked on a business career. He redeemed himself in many ways and is now considered a hero in his home country.

As a *Wired Differently* person I discover myself not knowing when to quit. After watching Durán I found myself applauding him. True, he was far from a perfect human being, but he was a warrior. He had put himself in an emotionally charged situation and did what he had to do.

As *Wired Differently* people, we take this stuff seriously. We need to understand that pulling out of a bad position can be part of the process in becoming a better person. The development of a

Wired Differently person is to remove *I quit* from their vernacular and instead embrace the concept of *No Mas*.

Where do we start?

A *Wired Differently* person starts by saying *No Mas* to the head trash churning in their minds. No more negative thoughts. No more angst. *I'm drawing a line in the sand. No Mas.*

As I'm writing this, the country is consumed with what happened to George Floyd and what his murder means to all of us. Sadly, this is not the first time we've seen police brutality and then suffered race riots. I remember the Rodney King riots in Los Angeles. I remember the fear that gripped everyone, especially the terror of watching Reginald Denny dragged from his truck and beaten. He'd been attacked by black gangsters because he was white. I have to add that he was rescued by local black residents who wrestled him from the violent mob and drove him to the hospital.

We all suffer the consequences of racism. We need to say no more to racism. No more to inequality. No more to what's not working for us as a society. *No Mas!*

What can we do?

To begin, we must consider the other side. Why is it that they're not happy? Why is it that they're frustrated with their situation?

Every great leader knows the value of negotiation, and the key to successful negotiation is empathy and understanding what the other side is thinking. There is no way you have all the answers and conversely, no way the other side has all the answers.

What has made me successful in many endeavors is my willingness to engage the other side. Not just in business, but in all aspects of my life.

I'm going to give you three examples to show you what I mean.

***

Las Vegas, Nevada

I was in Las Vegas for a business conference and decided I needed to touch up my shoes to add a little more sparkle to my professional appearance. I stopped at a shoeshine stand along the sidewalk and climbed into the chair.

As the shoeshine man, an elderly black individual, got busy on my shoes, I tried to lose myself in a newspaper. Truth is, I've never been comfortable with someone else shining my shoes, especially outdoors like this in public.

I said, "Stop."

He looked up at me. "Yes, sir. Is there a problem?"

The problem was that I felt wrong. Why did I feel strange about myself as I was looking down at him while he was shining my shoes? I knew why I was here. I wanted to know why he was here at this particular time. I told him, "Excuse me, sir. I want to switch places."

He looked at me with skepticism. "What are you talking about?"

"I want you to sit in this chair."

"Why?"

"I want to shine your shoes."

"You're crazy."

"I'm not crazy. I'm paying for your time, so please, sit in this chair."

He climbed into the seat and planted his shoes on the footrests.

I knelt below his feet and looked at the shoeshine implements. "What do I do?"

"You start with the rag and the soapy water."

"Okay, I got it." I went to town on his shoes, which were a pair of sneakers, covered with grime, which I scrubbed until they were clean. As I toiled, I thought about his life shining shoes and what it was like being a black man all this time.

When I got those shoes as spotless as I could get them, I asked, "How do they look?"

He studied them, a slight smile on his face. "Pretty good for tennis." He stared at me. "Why are you doing this?"

"Because," I admitted, "I didn't like you shining my shoes. The situation made me uncomfortable. I want to know, why are you doing this while I'm doing something else. You and I had different starts in life, I'm assuming. Here I am and here you are. Why?"

He blinked at me.

"I'm just trying to understand," I explained. "I want to know the other side."

"What exactly do you want to know?"

The question was hard to ask but I did it anyway. "What's it really like to be a black man in this country?"

"I tell you what I know and what I've seen," he began. He shared what he'd experienced under the different presidents, Johnson to Nixon to Carter to Reagan, Bush. Some of his stories seemed logical given the circumstances of the time and others were quite bizarre. But were they?

My takeaway from that episode was: Are we willing to confront our own injustices, our prejudices, our biases… Are we willing to say, *No Mas!*

***

Los Angeles, California

I was on another business trip and this time my wife accompanied me. It was the 1990s, and a typical day in downtown Los Angeles where we had to navigate around the homeless and panhandlers crowding the sidewalk.

I found myself judging and dismissing them by asking myself, why don't they get cleaned up and find a job? I became frustrated with all these people asking me for money while I worked hard for mine. Every dollar in my wallet, I had earned; no one had given it to me. He was faking. The usual *blah, blah, blah.*

That was when I had a *No Mas* moment.

I told my wife to go to the mall because I had to do something.

"What?"

I pointed to a corner. "I'm going over there and see what it's like to be a beggar."

She gave me one of her exclusive, *Todd, you're nuts* looks, then disappeared into the store.

I took off my shirt and turned it inside out. One of the panhandlers was taking a break in the shade of a traffic signal pole. I made a sign from a discarded cardboard box and took his place. My plan was that I'd stay at this corner until I'd begged $20.

The task was more difficult than I expected. I found myself on the receiving end of those judgmental stares that avert just as we make eye contact. I could read their thoughts. *Why doesn't he get a job? Faker! Loser!*

As I stood there, my thoughts churned on how the answer wasn't as straightforward as simply going to work. Some people aren't wired to work. They have problems fitting in socially. They might have substance abuse problems. Others are mentally challenged. True, a few take advantage of the system, but not that many.

What was hard for me was asking for money. I knew that those I was panhandling had toiled for their money and why should they give it to me? I didn't want to lie and say that I needed the money to buy food. But I did need this money to help me understand what the homeless go through.

A passerby finally stopped and looked me over. "You really need the money?"

"Yes, I do. I'm in a bad way. I'm trying to understand some things."

He reached into his pocket. "Here's a twenty. I hope things get better for you."

I thanked him. In a weird way, his act of generosity helped complete my circle.

I had to experience shining shoes. I had to experience what it was like to submerge myself into the role of being a beggar. But there was another circumstance that I had to experience, one that I could not simply volunteer to do.

———

*"There are only Two Types of Makes in Life: Make progress...or Make excuses." -**Todd Saylor***

———

***

Angola, Indiana

I used to look at people who got arrested as they deserved it. How do you accidentally get arrested? How do you not realize what you're doing? Given this attitude, I never understood what it was like to be persecuted by the system until I got arrested.

The episode stemmed from an altercation with a neighbor. He and I had bad chemistry on account that he had been mean to me and even to my kids. He resented me because I was a wealthy businessman with "soft hands" while he was a farmer. Furthermore, I'd unknowingly bought twenty acres of his family's homestead.

Normally, I gave him a wide berth, but I needed his signature on a form to acknowledge that I'd given him notice about a party I was organizing. We were planning our fifth fireworks show and the fire department needed that form before I could get the go-ahead.

I called his house and he told me that we could meet at a local auto garage. I drove there and found him outside. Reluctantly, he signed the form and when he handed it over, he called me a name. Much larger than me, he hit me, knocking my sunglasses off and popping my head against the side of my truck. In reflex, I hit him back and when I saw that he stepped toward me again, I hit him again, more powerfully this time.

The altercation ended, but since I knew this might not end well, I drove to the police station and submitted a written report to explain what had happened. The police officer looked it over and said he didn't see that I'd get in trouble. The days passed without incident until the week before the fireworks party, when a little birdie in the courthouse called my wife to say that a warrant was being prepared for my arrest. My wife couldn't get hold of me so she called an attorney, who when he did contact me, advised that I go to Michigan. However, I wasn't going to add fleeing arrest to the charges so I said the police could come get me when they were ready. As it turned out, I was to turn myself in the following Monday. That weekend I hosted the party, and even though I had an arrest warrant, the cops were there in case my neighbor arrived to cause trouble.

Monday, dressed in a suit and tie, I reported to the police station. I was escorted to the jail, where I got my mug shot and was told to wait for my appearance before the judge. The detective said, "Mr. Saylor, sit over there. You don't have to wait in the holding cell."

Several men in orange jumpsuits were already in the holding cell, waiting their turn before the judge. I didn't want preferential treatment, so I said, "Put me in the jail cell."

The detective ignored me. For two hours I sat there. Then a large police officer approached the cell and unlocked the door. Using his most authoritative voice, he barked, "Ramirez!"

A Hispanic man stood and approached. The cop shackled his wrists and ankles and ran a chain between them.

The cop barked again, "Sanchez!"

Another Hispanic man stepped forward and he was shackled and chained.

Then another Hispanic was called. And another. As the cop went down the line, I watched, amazed, at the criminal justice system in action.

Finally, the last name was called. "Saylor!"

Saylor. What?

"Todd Saylor!"

In disbelief, I stood and answered. With no deference as to who I was, the cop pulled me to the end of the line and chained me like he had done to everyone else.

"Let's go, men," he said, to begin our trek from the jail to the courthouse. The shackles and chains kept us from taking regular steps, so we proceeded in a humiliating shuffle, the infamous perp walk as if we were all serial killers.

While I was lost in an introspective funk, the other guys were excited to be outside. They took their time crossing the hundred yards to the courthouse, me at the end of the line, the only guy in a suit. I stuck out, definitely the odd one, all right.

Passing cars honked at us. The shame of people pointing and laughing at me was something I never thought would happen. But for many people, this is a big part of their life. Some of it deserved. Some of it not. I'm not trying to make excuses for someone else's behavior.

We were processed through the hearing and when that was finished, I asked the others if I could get at the front of the line.

"*Sí.* You can do that."

We were again shackled and chained. Once outside, I raced down that path back to the jail. Our guard yelled, "Halt!"

I shouted back to him, "Catch me if you can." I must have set the record for the hundred-meter perp-walk shuffle. After reaching the jail, I bailed myself out and helped a couple of my fellow inmates. They'd been put in jail for small offenses, and it didn't seem right for them to be locked up for want of money. I did what I could and even provided testimony for one.

———

"Waste no time arguing about what a good man should be. Be one."
-Marcus Aurelius

———

***

Certainly, my three experiences can't measure up in a significant way to what others have tolerated their entire lives, but I've been on the other side, either voluntarily or coerced by the system.

As *Wired Differently* people, are we willing to understand what other people are suffering through? Poverty? Injustice? Racism? Persecution? Abuse? Bias?

Or do we simply sit back, pull the curtains around us, and enjoy what we have?

Or do we as *Wired Differently* people say, no more. *No mas!*

Are we going to look at corner panhandlers and ask, why are they faking it? Or are we going to show empathy? Are we willing to understand what it's like to be discriminated against or persecuted because you stood up for yourself?

As *Wired Differently* people, are we willing to embrace our *No Mas* moments? Are we willing to proclaim and follow through with *No More!*

No—No more DriftAgain surprises.

M—Make progress or make excuses.

A—Analyze yourself, then really analyze yourself.

S—Seek before you peak.

———

"Do not be overcome by evil but overcome evil with good."

-Romans 12:21

———

CHAPTER EIGHT

THE OWN

*"Sometimes you have to lose who you are to become who you want to be." -**Todd Saylor***

In this book, I've stressed the importance of the link between what it means to be *Wired Differently* and the concept *of DriftAgain*, a key component if we want to be *Supremely Purposeful*. If we are to be *Wired Differently* then we must "OWN" all aspects of who we are and what we can be.

Wired Differently people understand that they can't be without bias or flaws or think that they had a perfect upbringing. *Wired Differently* people are overcomers for this reason. They use their attitudinal disorder to reconcile their flaws with their ambitions and thus triumph over their shortcomings and limits. Being *Wired Differently* is defined by what we are willing to give up, to become who we want to be.

The idea behind "who we are and who we want to be" is crucial to understanding the Own. We must find out who we are, what our genetics are, and understand how that affects our innate thought processes. Then as *Wired Differently* people we must rewire our minds to overcome the *DriftAgain*, focusing on becoming *Supremely Purposeful*.

In trying to understand *Supremely Purposeful*, I have to take a look at the world that we live in today, my land and my means. We're in the middle of a pandemic and dealing, once again, with racism. Across the country, riots have incinerated entire city blocks. Homelessness is rampant. Unemployment is at the highest levels of my lifetime. Our country hasn't been in such bad straits since the Great Depression and World War Two.

Here's the strange part. When I compare what I'm living through to the anxiety of the 1930s and the early '40s, it feels so different than what I feel that it should. The reason is that my impression of the Great Depression and World War Two comes from those black-and-white images we're so familiar with. But what we're living through is in living color, it's real. We're experiencing the totality of what's going on and it doesn't seem as bad. We forget that during the Great Depression, most people were working. Then during World War Two, here in the US, life continued. The fear of an enemy attack was mostly due to paranoia and hysteria. And presently, that paranoia and hysteria make a return as we confront a new and very real, invisible threat.

What does this have to do with the idea of Owning? It's that you have to own your situation. You have to own yourself. You have to own responsibility. You have to own the era. You have to own the decisions you make in dealing with your world, all of which is in living color. Now.

The manner in which we "Own" can be broken down into these three points:

One. Understand the definition at the core of being *Wired Differently*, which is to overcome some, if not even much, of our innate self.

Two. Recognize that living as our innate self has its distinct rituals and habits that are hard-wired into our minds. When we come together as *Wired Differently* people, we have to recognize that the commonality and likeness of our being *Wired Differently* is that we have to overcome our innate self to become *Supremely Purposeful*. It's not that our innate self is all bad, it's that to achieve the success that we want, we have to overcome some of our inherited beliefs and traits, our natural genetic wiring, and our attitudinal disorder. We need to see the other side.

Three. Understand that by the time we're 12 years old, we've been shaped and honed by our parents, that we've been molded according to our attitudinal disorder. A *Wired Differently* person embraces that one of their most important personality traits is their ability to break free of early thoughts, of early unfounded premises, to unravel their wiring that has been set in place since infancy and adolescence to achieve their Supremely Purposeful being.

The pull of our Innate Self

Becoming a *Wired Differently* person is to overcome our innate self and create a distinct *Wired Differently* self in our quest to be *Supremely Purposeful*. What makes this so challenging is that we inherited many beliefs during our childhood, mostly from our family and particularly from our parents.

You have to acknowledge that just because your father did things one way, and your grandfather did the same things, doesn't mean you have to. And you can't. Because times change. Expectations change. Society changes. Technology changes. For example, to this day my dad, as amazing as he is, won't use a computer because he says he doesn't believe in them. He still uses a flip phone and makes carbon copies. If I used those, I couldn't be functional in modern business.

Which brings me to another amazing man, Nik Wallenda, the famous high-wire acrobat. His life was steeped in the family's culture that began with his great-grandfather, Karl Wallenda.

Many in his family have created a version of the high-wire act, which I know you've heard of as The Flying Wallendas. Though Nik and his family are famous as wire walkers, they, like most of us, have extensive and varied resumés that have led them to their present accomplishments. They prove that it takes years to become an "overnight success."

I first met Nik in 2014 at a speaking engagement for which I had hired him for a fundraiser. We quickly established a rapport and became friends. What drew us to each other was that we recognized that we were both strong Christians and we each highly respected the other's achievements. I admired his willingness to seek out exciting, death-defying escapades that pushed the envelope of what most people considered absolutely terrifying.

Here's what I learned about Nik. He considered himself foremost as a performer, an acrobat as dedicated to his craft as any professional musician or actor. And like most artists on their way to establishing themselves, he needed a day job to pay the bills. For many years in his early adult life, he was the general manager of a busy restaurant, which gave him plenty of experience handling cash flow, scheduling, inventory, and the typical headaches of dealing with customers, employees, vendors, and the government.

I discovered that what attracted him to me was that I'm an entrepreneur. He respected my willingness to risk my money and time, but not my life, in my quest to lead companies and change things.

Picture two guys sitting at a Starbucks becoming friends by embracing each other's fears. I drew inspiration in that he could walk across a wire strung over Niagara Falls and another time, the Grand Canyon. His performance epitomized a nerves-of-steel bravery that astounded me.

Nik admitted to me it was easier for him to risk his life than his money, and that despite his ability to walk a wire at outlandish heights, he was apprehensive about stepping out on other entrepreneurial risks, of literally stepping off the wire and expanding his business from where it had been mostly produced by others. He'd started this before, exercising his entrepreneurial craft by developing the high-wire act from what he considered a dying brand, transforming it from an old-time circus attraction to something more original and dynamic. Now he was ready to build on what he had learned but looked for encouragement and wisdom.

Just as Nik was fearful at the prospect of stepping away from his entrepreneurial comfort zone, I too was fearful of jumping out of a plane or of doing anything Nik was famous for such as walking on a wire strung high above the ground.

He and I came to understand that our fears mirrored each other's. We continued this conversation back and forth until 2018 when I challenged him with this concept of stepping outside his *Land of Quo*. The irony was obvious. He was the world's greatest wire walker—super successful and wealthy in that regard—but despite his fame, he was really in the "Land of Quo *Pro*" because he was already successful and famous for walking wires. That situation is not uncommon for accomplished people such as professional actors and athletes. Tom Brady may be the greatest quarterback in the world and even with his competitive spirit and drive, can he do anything more? Just because he's successful in football doesn't mean that he isn't locked into a solid win at everything.

Actors get stale. Athletes get stale. They get branded as this certain character who exists within this certain zone. Likewise, Nik felt that he had possibly fallen into the same routine.

I encouraged him to get out of his *Land of Quo Pro* by stretching his leadership palette and to think beyond walking on wire and into more entrepreneurial leadership roles. He had to risk more to gain more.

Easier said than done. You must understand that asking Nik Wallenda, the most fearless man alive, to risk his own money was more daunting to him than risking his life. His past as a performer had been what he described as either "eating chicken or feathers," another way of saying feast or famine.

I encouraged Nik to embrace his "fear of feathers" and so risk his money to become the empowered person he keenly deserved to be, not only as an event producer and company CEO, but as the author of his full entrepreneurial destiny.

Nik and I discussed that the culture he learned was "a fear of the feathers, the fear of being impoverished." It's what drove him to stay in this Land of Quo Pro, to limit himself to be a performer; to do otherwise meant the possibility of eating feathers and no more chicken. Although great at walking wires, he felt this burning desire that he could do more.

Nik knew that even though he might be the greatest wire walker in the world, to get to whatever the next thing was in his life, he had to keep taking the next step. We can get mired in the *Land of Quo* by this tunnel-vision of possibly being impoverished, or losing steam in our endeavors, or from the inertia of our daily grind, an attitude known as the *Law of Lack*.

As hard as this may be to believe, when I explained to him that I felt he was actually a better businessman than a wire walker, Nik's "glow" for entrepreneurship seemed to be really percolating. Though he had experience in the business side of circus performing, he had bigger plans to do things as an entrepreneur. Prior to this, he'd mostly worked with managers from Dick Clark Productions, ABC, NBC, and Discovery Channel, and other large event underwriters. You would think a dream to most, but not always, exactly, to Nik.

You see, I've watched Nik as he's literally reengineered these very big events and overcome countless problems, re-imagined their ideas, changed wardrobes, protected his workers, managed security, included his friends; re-rig cabling, buy everyone meals, then walk the wire—*all in the very same day!*

Nik is truly spectacular, and our conversation was going great. He ultimately decided on launching his own circus, when the Covid pandemic hit. Suddenly, his plans, like everyone else's, were jolted to a halt. At this point, I have to congratulate him on his guts and remarkable business savvy. Instead of marking time and waiting for circumstances so he could proceed with his circus, he said, "I'm not going to wait for this Covid to be over, and I'm going to continue in my own way." By acting on these words, he was overcoming his innate self of staying on the safer financial route. Choosing between chicken and feathers was no longer part of the equation.

Within three weeks Nik created and produced the first ever in the world of social distancing, *The Nik Wallenda Daredevil Rally Drive-In Thrill Show*, featuring not just himself, but acts from all over the world, which were performed in front of cars parked outside the Florida Sarasota UTC Mall. He sold out crowds for many weeks straight, giving an opportunity for other performers to bust out in this time of social distancing. Next, in the second run of the *Daredevil Rally*, I was offered the opportunity of marketing it as *The Nik Wallenda Daredevil Rally presents: Wired Differently!* To which I said, "Yes! Absolutely. What a thrill."

It was also especially enriching and empowering to see Nik step out and be the impresario he wanted to be, to see him overcome the innate fear that still lingers since his great-grandfather fell off a wire and to go on and be the first ever to walk across an active volcano. Nik even wrote a book addressing this: *Facing Fear*. I'll bet you that overcoming his family's innate reluctance and doubts was as difficult for him as it would be for me to wire-walk like Nik. It's a privilege and a blast to be involved in this great family of the Wallenda, Wired Differently Warriors. With them, I learned much during each and every moment as they encompassed life, business, and spirit. Thanks, Wallendas.

———

*"We all have volcanos we have to walk across." -***Todd Saylor**

———

I have my own innate "feathers" that I have to overcome.

My grandfather drove for Standard Oil and prided himself as an exemplary worker in a time when there were more workers than bosses. They didn't have many opportunities to branch out so there was not much of an entrepreneurial spirit.

My dad watched his father work for forty years straight and never miss a day, was never late, and considered himself a solid employee doing an honest day's work for a fair wage. When my grandfather retired in his mid-sixties, he was presented with a gold watch as a tribute for his decades of forthright service.

I was about ten when my grandfather died and I thought about what he had accomplished, which had been providing in hard times a nice home for his wife and children. In relating this family history, my father was ingraining within me this ethic of working a steady job for forty years, getting the gold watch, and in the process, giving my family what they needed.

My dad's appreciation of the value and significance of such principles was likewise ingrained into him when at the age of 14, his father told him that he needed a job. That summer, my dad left home with five other local boys to live in a trailer making donuts at Indian Lake, Ohio. This was my dad's summer vacation until he was 18 years old.

In sharing these stories, these principles were being passed on, my grandfather to my dad, my dad to me. *Do your job. Show up on time. Be accountable.* These are admirable traits, don't get me wrong, traits necessary for success in any endeavor. Along with these, my father taught me many other great things which is why I write about him all the time. But with that, what he was also wiring into my brain was this idea of getting a gold watch. *Keep that same job. Do the hard work. Keep that momentum. Play it safe.*

Nik Wallenda was going to get his gold watch by walking across a wire. I was going to get my gold watch by being a Steady Eddie, working one job while doing a one-employee role. Going through the paces and sticking to my path.

But there was another trait that was passed down these three generations. And that was, *Don't get too far in front of your skis. Don't dream too big. Don't risk too much. Don't spend money. Don't talk about yourself. Don't demonstrate things that are too far out there because what happens if you fail?* It was the *Law of Lack* speaking through my father and grandfather.

However, the idea of working for someone drove me crazy. But how do you get a gold watch if you don't work for somebody else? Maybe—and this idea hit me like a bolt of lightning—maybe I didn't want that gold watch. That realization planted in me this notion of moving away from who I was to who I needed to be.

From my childhood, I knew I wanted to be in sales, I wanted to be an entrepreneur, and I wanted to be working for myself. I knew I wanted to do those things because my father was like that, parts of his life anyway. He was a teacher, but he also ran a donut shop as a side business. I had no interest in becoming a teacher, but what attracted me was this donut shop that my dad wasn't paying much attention to.

Since I worked at the shop, I was aware of how much money we could make selling donuts. I used to think, why is my dad teaching for pennies when he could be making epic gains in the donut business? When I asked him that question, he replied, "We need security, son."

I pressed him, "What do you mean, security?"

He said, "We need the security of a steady paycheck every week."

"Dad, it's not very much compared to what we can do in this business."

"Son, you don't get it. It's security. It's a paycheck you can count on."

My dad was speaking from his *Law of Lack*. For me to follow my dreams, to act upon being Wired Differently, I had to unshackle myself from one part of the Saylor family's principles and break out of my *Land of Quo*.

Even to this day, when I do a Facebook post, or when I announce with a big splash the plans for my next business, or when I speak and motivate people about things that can be done or that I've done, I feel that tug binding me to my family's principles. What will my father say or think?

For several years now I've been getting on stage and telling people: *Believe, Prepare, Attack*, and to back that up, to prove that I've lived up to what I've been preaching, I'm somewhat required to say, "I'm a millionaire." But talking about myself this way still feels like I'm pulling my own teeth. Every time I talk about myself or discuss my business, I feel my dad's questioning stare. I've gone so far as to change the back-cover copy of *Wired Differently* from "self-made millionaire" to "team-made millionaire" to draw attention away from myself. Yes, I am a self-made millionaire, by definition, but it took the efforts of many. However, my psyche wouldn't let me write that because I was afraid that my dad would see it. That's how strong these innate principles pulled at me.

Even now with wealth, I still work at: How can I present myself? How can I share these things? How can I do these things? To do that, I have to talk about myself. For me to build credibility, I have to share about my good and my bad. Yet the innate dialogue haunts me.

Son, don't think too big. The more you talk about your intentions, the bigger chance you have to fail. People are going to judge you as a failure. Don't take that risk.

Things are going too good for you. You can't always be successful. You know the other shoe is going to drop soon. It won't be good forever.

Growing up hearing that, I got so sick of it. Now that I'm 55 years old and well into my own career, cataloging successes and overcoming one big obstacle after another, when I sit with my dad, the first thing he says is, "Have you thought about this happening? Have you thought about that?"

This is the whole concept of lack speaking though him, something he's shared with me his entire life. You can spend your time planning for bad things that probably never happen.

"Worrying is betting against yourself." -**Alex Bova**

Or you can spend your time on how you're going to invest your money, your success, your progress, and what you can share with your family. You're either going to live in lack mentality or you're going to live in success mentality.

Part of being successful in business is that you must be willing to promote yourself and your ideas, which is another way of saying, how you talk about yourself. Listen, please, to this point:

My brand has never made me a penny, but my principles have made me millions.

There's a need, however, to balance ego-empathy. *Wired Differently* people realize they have an ego and that's not a bad thing. The ego, our sense of worth and ability, is a powerful dynamic force that propels us. If we can keep our ego in check, and not succumb to narcissism and its self-defeating behaviors, then we can become unstoppable.

You can become a ferocious leader. But you must also have the right ego-empathy balance to pull it off. You can't be all ego and feel that the world revolves around you. And you can't be all empathy either, meaning you can't go around feeling sorry for everyone all the time and not have enough ego to drive the process to help them or yourself. But you can't be so egotistical that all you concern yourself with is status, admiration, and money, and in acquiring that, you step on whomever you have to step on to get what you think you want. Do that and you won't have a long career. Ego-empathy balance is the key to this aspect of *Wired Differently* personalities and this idea of leaving who we are to become who we want to be.

To be part of the *Wired Differently* culture is to understand that though you were born to certain means, you have the ability to grow in any direction to be Supremely Purposeful. When someone decides to question your plans, you say, "I'm going to go ahead and build that company. And I'm going to do a million in sales the next two years."

And they counter, "Who told you that you could say that?"

"Todd Saylor said that. He said that if I raise my V&R, and am supremely purposeful about it, it will happen. Raising your Volume will raise your Reps and you will accomplish what you've set out to achieve."

And then they will reply, "Todd Saylor got you to believe that? It's not going to happen."

"I believe him."

You have the right to tell that doubting Thomas that these are your dreams, your visions, your thoughts. You have the right to say, "I believe him over you. I supremely believe in my dreams. I supremely believe that I can make these things happen."

It is you who has the power to say *NO*. You can say *No* to your mom. *No* to your dad. *No* to your teacher. *No* to your boss. You can say *No* to the President of the United States. That's what makes this the greatest country in the world. You have the freedom to say *No* to anyone.

You even have the right to say No to God! In reply, He says, "Okay. I've given you free will."

You've been saying No to authority figures all your life. So why is it hard to say No to a naysayer?

The Own is this willingness to leave yourself behind, follow your dreams, to resist the *DriftAgain*, and to be *Supremely Purposeful* in thought and action. This is being *Wired Differently*, this ability to lose who we are to become who we want to be.

Before you start on that path, you have to know what you want.

Can you answer that question?

Only five out of a hundred people in America are successful. But only those five people can answer the question of knowing what they want, what they want to *own*.

I want you to OWN.

O—Obsess Supremely Purposely.

W—Win each Purposeful Thought.

N—Never yield to the Law of Lack.

———

*"God has not given us a spirit of fear and timidity, but of power, love, and self-discipline." -2 **Tim. 1: 7***

———

CONCLUSION

As a *Wired Differently* person, you're constantly evaluating yourself and learning more about who you are, and this is how we find our truth. We know that our lives are a constant struggle against the *Drift* and the *DriftAgain* as those pull us relentlessly toward the *Land of Quo*. But our efforts are not in vain because we have these eight overcomer traits we must harness if we are to resist the *Drift*:

1. DriftAgain: We all, and especially *Wired Differently* people, keep drifting again, often because of the same weakness.
2. The MARK: Pegging your efforts to compete against a specific person.
3. The EGO: Acknowledging Empathy-Ego Balance.
4. The VIEW: Our perception of the world.
5. The PAIN: Welcome the pain.
6. The ODD: Dare to be different.
7. NO MAS: Give yourself permission to say *No More!*
8. The OWN: Be willing to lose who you are to be who you want to be.

***

Being Wired Differently will lead you to discuss your favorite topic and my favorite topic, which is: ME. And in discussing *ME*, meaning yourself, then you must get at the whole truth about yourself.

The first thing to understand about yourself is that you are an individual. You are not to be compared to anyone else. If you get caught up comparing yourself to others, you lose focus on your individuality and being the best in the world in your craft.

But you may ask, Todd, didn't you tell us to find a *MARK*? Someone to use as a benchmark to gauge our efforts as we strive for success?

Remember that the *MARK* represents your competition. And you compete by leveraging your favor as an individual. You have to find your own channel. You have to create your own life. Dare to be *ODD*. You have to find your own way, leverage your individuality and become harmonious in your life.

As I was growing up, more than anything else, I wanted to play in the NFL. But in college I realized that might not happen. I had to change that narrative. I had to change my perception of the world, I had to change my *VIEW*.

To accomplish that, I sat down and said to myself, *Todd, you've got to get serious about your grades. You've got to change who you are to become who you want to be.* From that point on, I acted upon my *EGO*. I started carrying my books around. I started standing a little straighter. I started dressing a little smarter. I started sitting in the front row. The more I acted like a serious student, the more I became a serious student.

What happened? My grades improved. People started deferring to me. I was treated like someone who had a lot on the ball.

———

*"For as he thinketh in his heart, so he is." -**Proverbs 23:7***

———

Then in my senior year, it was clear my football career was over. I could no longer attach my self-worth to the thought of playing professional football. This was a *No Mas* moment. I had to choose another path, another channel. Fortunately, my earlier decision to focus on my business studies helped direct me into this new career. To move ahead, we must *OWN* what we want, and the price for me was giving up what I thought was destined to be. It's never easy as we have to make lots of sacrifices and my reaction to that anguish is what led to my entrepreneurial success. If it were easy and without *PAIN*, then we wouldn't need to be *Wired Differently*, and everybody would be doing it.

You've got to be willing to dig deep into yourself so you can find, develop, and share your gifts with the rest of the world to establish that *Empathy-Ego Balance*.

You must move into a lane where you can focus on being the best in the world at your craft whether it's as a housewife, a doctor, a teacher, a donut maker, a payroll guy, a manufacturer, a farmer.

You're an elite and deserve to be treated as such. Remember that!

Our Creator of infinite intelligence has yielded to you a specific purpose, one you will fulfill by being *Supremely Purposeful.*

***

To be *Supremely Purposeful* begins with the *MIND*. Your mind is constantly churning with the consciousness, which is your streaming thoughts analyzing your experiences, beliefs, and reactions by what your subconscious is telling you.

The subconscious is the piece of your mind that's embedded with the emotions that you've accumulated throughout your life. People said things about you that were not true, and you believed it in your consciousness. You've got to rewire those thoughts (*Wired Differently!*) and deal with the fact that you've consumed untruths about yourself and you've got to flush them out so you can deal with them. Taming your subconscious is the key to your freedom. Your subconscious will express to the world that you are *Wired Differently*: confident, focused, disciplined.

———

*"Desire is the starting point of all achievement." -**Napoleon Hill***

———

Elect to direct our consciousness into our subconsciousness. We do that by molding our consciousness with these six plays: Obtain; Attend; Listen; Cultivate; Associate; and Expose.

Number 1: Obtain. Go and obtain a good book, one that inspires and teaches wisdom. Let's start with the Bible and specifically Psalms 23:7. *What a person thinks in their heart so are they.* The heart is your subconscious. So, what you think in your heart is you.

Number 2: Attend. I want you to attend positive lectures. I need you to surround yourself with positive lecturers. Their positive messages are bulwarks against all the negativity that surrounds us constantly.

Number 3: Listen. One of my secrets is to listen, but listen well, meaning to positive and confident teachers. Listen to their live lectures and their recordings. Listening comes naturally to us humans since our distant ancestors gathered around a fire to be entranced by a good story. Listening is one of the best ways to understand. Listen inductively.

Number 4: Cultivate. I want you to cultivate friends who have self-confidence. Seek out opportunities to make friends with such people.

Number 5: Associate. I want you to associate with people of high character. Remember that you can judge a man by the company he keeps.

Number 6. Expose. It sounds comical when I tell you to expose yourself but what I mean is to expose yourself to every possible source regarding the study of your mental process. It's incumbent on you to do this so you can better the lives of other people.

***

Wired Differently people can't separate business from life and the challenge is to make our efforts harmonious regarding our work, ourselves, and our relationships.

God made you each an individual so that you make your own decisions, choose your own life, and get anything in the world that you want. You can do such in this great country of America. Let's do this thing called Life, of being *Wired Differently*.

As I concluded this book, it dawned on me how much I want to encourage you, how proud I am of you and your commitment to the readings and bettering of yourself and bettering of others. In this final chapter I want you to desire the secret truths of life and the success of being Wired Differently.

———

"Writing a book is forever. It seems to take forever, but it actually only lasts forever." -**Todd Saylor**

———

The most important concept I want to tell every reader in every chapter, always, again and again, are these four words:

———

You can do it.

———

You really can do it. You are truly *Wired Differently* and can accomplish things that are immeasurably and abundantly possible beyond your immediate comprehension. Romans 3:20 assures us of this, and you need to hear it over and over again.

So you must—I desperately beg you to—

BELIEVE BIGGER, PREPARE BIGGER, ATTACK BIGGER.

Originally, when I wrote those last words of this chapter, I thought I was done with this book. Then it was time to work on the cover when this revelation burst upon me, screaming, *You're not yet done, Todd! You need the perfect image for the book!*

Easy enough you say. And so I thought as well.

The Final Purposeful Story - Cover story, Part 1:

However, I wasn't off to a great start. I'd come down with covid and had just finished my quarantine. Although I'd been given a clean bill of health, I still wasn't feeling a hundred percent. But I continued forward.

For the cover, I had this image in my head in which I hoisted a staff across my shoulders as I waded into the ocean to climb upon a large boulder. I wanted the photo to be a metaphor for living a Supremely Purposeful life as a *Wired Differently* person.

I began my search for the perfect setting around Anna Marie Island, close to my Florida home. After scouting the beach, I found the ideal place on the third island near Longboat Key, which ended up being directly west of my house, a mile or so across the bay.

From my balcony, the vista is breathtaking, facing directly across the open water towards Mexico, a scene of utmost serenity as the surf laps against the sand and rocks. But that impression can be deceptive as it's also the spot where I nearly drowned, an incident I described in Chapter 1 of my first book, *Wired Differently*.

Upon returning home, I asked my wife, Traci, "Hey babe, can you come with me to do a practice photo shoot?"

"Sure, when?" she replied.

"Now, I'm excited. Let's go."

Traci laughed and replied in *her are you kidding me voice*, "It's not that easy. We have Saylor." She pointed toward our six-year-old grandson. "Plus, I'm busy."

"C'mon," I insisted. "It's not far. Bring Saylor, it will be fun."

Her begrudging response was, "Todd, why do you do things like this?"

After 32 years of being married to a *Wired Differently* person, she still has to ask?

I didn't answer, only saying, "Let me grab some water and gear."

With Saylor in tow, we packed into the car and drove to the island point, the location of the isolated rock on the tip of what locals call Beer Can Island, actually named Greer Island.

We were among the few people out there as the beach was undergoing erosion rehab and the sky was darkening because of an approaching storm. As there wasn't much time to get these practice shots, my mind was full with questions. Where could it possibly work? What would the image look like? How could I possibly capture my vision and emotions in the short moments before the wind picked up and brought rain? Strangely, though I felt hurried, outwardly the moment seemed quite calm.

The tide was rolling in and the waves were mounting. As I said to my wife, "Honey, start taking pictures. The rain is coming," I picked up a big piece of driftwood the perfect length of staff. Its weathered appearance represented the idea that I wanted to portray, of triumphing over adversity, of being *Supremely Purposeful*. "Babe, capture me on the way to this rock again. I have to see what it looks and feels like to stand on the rock with this driftwood."

The rock, seemingly a large outcropping of coral, maybe millions of years old, bristled with razor sharp edges. To stand on it was painful and dangerous, and I thought to myself:

———

"What did Christ's pain feel like?"

———

Of course, I could endure this discomfort again, to get it right before I dragged a film crew to this remote location.

Traci had taken a bunch of photos with her cell phone. However, the images were of low quality and besides, I was wearing surf shorts as I hadn't intended these photos to be anything more than a practice shoot for the actual cover.

In reviewing the photos, I found one to be especially inspirational and I was so moved that I posted that image on Facebook to announce this book and build anticipation for the final cover reveal.

But I had underestimated the impact of this photo upon me. My attempt to stir the winds and souls of others actually also caused mine to be swept away in a rush of spirit-filled emotion in connection with my Lord.

As much as I want God in my life, I still find myself Drifting Again and Again from Him. It's this lack of focus that holds us back from being Supremely Purposeful and massively successful, but even more damaging than that, is that the *DriftAgain* from our Lord keeps us from receiving His blessings and the rewards of His grace, mercy, and victories here on earth. The *DriftAgain* prevents us from being successful in our crafts and stifles our thoughts and dreams, hamstringing us from reaching our destinies and realizing a life of true joy.

I want you to understand that this extraordinary photo was possible because of the "Do it again instances" and from the "*DriftAgain* moments" that inspire us to grow. But I later learned that the photo represented another lesson about something beyond my control.

Cover story part 2:

Five days later I returned to that exact spot with the film crew. In the meantime, I'd thought at length about every detail to get the absolutely perfect cover image. This time, instead of surf shorts, I'd worn my *Wired Differently* stage clothing. What I wanted to present was the successful me struggling against the *DriftAgain* but triumphing by being Supremely Purposeful. I was certain we could easily recreate the practice shots and we'd be done.

Right away, things started to go wrong. First of all, in my post-covid condition, the 40-minute trek to the same spot as the practice shot exhausted me. In my mind, I saw us using the identical backdrop but to my surprise, the island point was gone, obliterated. The beach had been roped off and dredged, littered with piles of rocks. The state was constructing a jetty that transformed the shore and completely ruined my attempt to recreate the setting for what I hoped would be an epic photo.

Dismayed and disappointed, I decided to make the best of the circumstances and pressed on with the photo shoot. I looked about for a length of driftwood, searching for the ideal staff but all that I found were too big, too small, too long, too short, too heavy— none matched the one from the practice shoot. Plus, there was no solitary rock I could climb onto and so duplicate the moment of splendor and natural beauty from the original shoot.

Despite my misgivings, I picked up a piece of clumsy looking driftwood and headed toward the ocean. When I waded into the surf, I stepped on the pointed end of a tree stump buried in the sand, bruising the arch of my foot. Despite the discomfort, I soldiered on.

I yelled back to the photographer. "Now what?"

She shouted, "Keep moving, you look great!"

I look great?

I wanted an epic shot with the perfect staff and the perfect rock in my perfect *Wired Differently* clothing, not *You look great*.

Moreover, I didn't feel what we were doing was working. At the practice shoot, I could feel the Holy Spirit encompassing me, guiding my movements, making me flow with the moment.

This time, everything seemed contrived. The emotion behind this photo shoot felt forced, mechanical, unauthentic. But I wouldn't give up and knew that if we persisted, that we'd eventually find the perfect shot that I had in mind. The pain in my injured foot got worse and worse. For the next two hours, I hobbled in agony and the throbbing only subsided when standing in the cool sand of shallow water.

I yelled to the photographer, "Keep shooting. I'm wading into the deeper water. Get the waves crashing on me and my struggle to remain on my feet."

Click, click, click...then it happened.

A large wave, much bigger and more powerful than expected, heaved me up and then pulled me under. The staff was wrenched out of my grasp, and I was caught in the undertow. I rolled around in the sandy bottom, gathering my wits, and fought my way to the surface.

I emerged completely drenched: my entire body, my clothing, my jewelry, my watch, all soaked in salty ocean water. Everything was going wrong, and I felt foolish with nothing to show for this disaster. No picture of me hoisting the driftwood staff on my shoulders, no picture of me climbing the rock. What a waste of time.

Frustrated and angry, I stood and marched toward the break of the oncoming sea. To keep myself from giving up, I thought, *Todd, keep going. Don't be derailed. Keep pushing.*

———

Only you can inspire you.

———

Your message must be: Others need to know they must keep going regardless of the tide, the changing landscape, the lack of a prop. Just keep going, don't let the drift ruin you.

What came of that effort was the perfect cover shot, but one completely different than what I originally had in mind.

The practice photo presented me taking on the gift of the Crucifixion, acknowledging the ultimate triumph because of the ultimate sacrifice. That's what I wanted but what I got this time was a different portrayal, an amazingly and equally powerful homage to another of our Lord's gifts to us—that of the Baptismal, the sacrament of cleansing and the act of publicly admitting our acceptance of Jesus Christ as our Savior.

The photo I chose was of me rising from the ocean, dripping wet, in my good clothes, the moment raw and visceral. You couldn't avoid seeing what it meant: what I'd experienced was a Baptismal and that to be Supremely Purposeful is more than sacrifice; it is acceptance, of giving yourself over to something bigger than yourself, in this case to Jesus Christ.

In looking back at the difference between the practice and the final photos was an awareness that I had not seen the role that spontaneity and serendipity played in the shoots. It was as if God had said, *Get started and I will complete the task.*

My friends, at the heart of this revelation and the cover shoots is that:

"God's glory can't be recreated but can be created again and again Differently."

God's will occurs in real-time. He guides the moment and we need those moments to happen so we can move forward with Him. That's why the final cover photo was so amazing, stirring, and spiritually provoking, because it was a sublime point in time captured by the camera, demonstrating the real power of God's grace that keeps us pushing forward.

If we are *Wired Differently*, we must at all cost, in all ways, keep pushing forward again and again.

If we are Supremely Purposeful, we must understand that only we alone, can decide to move forward.

———

Only you can decide, to continue in your walk. -**Todd Saylor**

———

You see my friends, *Wired Differently* people do things again, and again, and drifting and sinning are behaviors our personalities keep repeating. People must know they will "*DriftAgain*" and so they have to "Repent again," then go "Do it again," to be "Successful Again."

When I hoisted the driftwood upon my shoulders or walked into the crashing waves, I thought, "Here I go again. Lord, I can do this. Here I go again."

During the practice shoot, I was well aware of the symbolism of the Crucifixion.

Then during the final shoot, when nothing was working according to my plan, I was willing to proceed anyway as I felt powered by the inertia of God's wisdom, that would lift me from the tide and inspire me to continue to plod forward.

The fact that Christ labored with the cross upon His shoulder, the fact that He plodded forward under all circumstances, that He was the example of the need for Baptism, of the public acceptance of His will are no coincidence to us *Wired Differently* people.

When we are Supremely Purposeful, we are aware that Christ was saying, "I'm going to 'do it again and again for you' because you will *DriftAgain*."

———

*"I will be there for you, I am your helper, I will never forsake you nor leave you for then what can man do to you." -**Hebrews 13:5***

———

Whatever you want in this world you can have, as the ultimate price has already been paid by Him. We have the Supremely Purposeful power to achieve it, that if we fall we can get back up, put on the full armor of God, heft that length of driftwood onto our shoulders, and march again into the unknown sea, and you do it again and again until you succeed.

Please pay attention here so that I'm perfectly clear about one of the greatest truths you will ever hear:

———

We are called to not be of this world, but to Overcome this world, in a Wired Differently way.

———

My job is to love you, inspire you, motivate you, encourage you, teach you, and to remind you that, YES, you can do it again.

Your job is to *Be, Do, and Think Differently Again and Again* and to never lose focus on God, to recover quickly from all *Drift-Agains* and remain Supremely Purposeful.

I've shared with you anecdotes of Supremely Purposeful moments and here at the closing, I find myself even more compelled to share the most important question you've ever been asked, which when answered will ignite the success within us in a manner that has never before been realized:

"Do you even know what you want?"

We will explore that question in my next book, *Supremely Purposeful*.

———

*"We have to be willing to change who we are, to become who we want to be." -**Todd Saylor***

———

ACKNOWLEDGEMENTS

While writing a book is a solitary endeavor, it is not the product of my efforts alone. Like success in life, I owe what's in this book to the contributions made to me by other people.

In Chapter 2, The Mark, I emphasized the need to find the Marks in your life and here are some of those Marks who helped me find success. Success doesn't have to be epic, in fact most successes are not, but they do have to happen often and be impactful. Here are some Marks of mine that I'm grateful for:

Traci Foltz Saylor: The most impressive person I've ever encountered. She is a daily Mark of humanity, beauty, and spirituality.

Phil Eberhart, RIP. My third through sixth grade PE teacher who taught me to enjoy competing and so gave me a vision of the man I wanted to be. Because of this, he is my first Leadership Mark.

Randy Darr. My childhood friend from birth who bested me in many athletic feats throughout my elementary years but always remained my best buddy. He was clearly a Mark before I knew what that concept was about.

Tom Saylor, my dad. I knew I could not be a complete man until I had equaled his accomplishments in life's long struggle.

Bruce Knox. My high-school secret athletic Mark and a friend whom I've long admired. While in college, through his actions in Big Brothers Big Sisters of America, he mentored a young man and upon graduating from Indiana University, Bruce continued to pay for and sponsor his "Little Brother" through college and into his career. Bruce's commitment through such an unselfish and unrecognized contribution to another person's well-being has moved me to this day and leads me to regard him as one of my Philanthropic Marks.

Rick Shipe: A high-school friend and clearly, an individual athletic competitive Mark. He and I dueled on the track and field team as pole vaulters for meet wins and to best the 20-year-old school record. After Rick eclipsed it first, I practiced using supremely purposeful efforts with him as my Mark to ultimately capture that record four times over.

Mrs. Aldrich: My sixth-grade English teacher. An exceptionally caring and firm person, she guided me, a new student in her school, to feel welcome and make new friends. Her balance of fairness, honesty, and criticism moved me to develop early leadership aspirations.

John Ludy: My wrestling coach who stayed after practice to wrestle me, using these grueling sessions to pound me without mercy in contests that pushed the boundaries of manhood with each ass-kicking. John is my Mark as an example of how to give tough love to others and remain a spectacularly genuine person.

Jeff Hinin: My first entrepreneurial Mark. Jeff built his printing company as I was struggling in my first donut shop. By taking in his example, I was convinced that I could achieve commercial success. Since then, I watched him blister his path and grow his business to massive levels.

Malcolm Kittrell: My first college football Mark as he was the perfect football specimen, a remarkable defensive player, and for three years, the upper-classman captain. I picked Malcolm as my early college football-conditioning Mark because I wanted to be noticed as a stand-out and to fulfill my captain aspirations. During my first college conditioning measures, I won recognition after he fought and pushed me to the finish in the mile race.

J.V. Gilbert: The ultimate football receiver and the Manchester University season record holder for touchdowns. J.V. pushed me to be better in football and in Christ. He was my Mark in football and in my Christian walk aspirations, actually steering me to God. Because of his mentorship of me, I quickly broke his record and to this day, as a preacher he boasts of his short record run as he witnesses and shares our exploits and the Gospel.

Wayne Wickard: Wayne pushed me to Grow and seek the Distance. My quote, "It's not just the efforts we make but more the distances we are willing to Go" was inspired through my ten years of mentorship revisit. Wayne's lasting Mark has served me in many ways as he drove me to evolve and learn to do things *Differently*. Wayne and I didn't agree on everything, but he gave me the opportunity to appreciate his business principles. Wayne has been one of my biggest entrepreneurial leadership and competitive business Marks.

Dean Kelly: My father's best friend and my local entrepreneur superstar Mark. Dean sold one of his businesses for eight figures and allowed me to shadow him and intern in that very company to learn how to be a success.

Delatorro McNeal II: The *Wired Differently* beginning Mark. Del is more than a friend, he is an exemplary example of a commitment to excellence. His Mark is to my own craft of excellence as we prepare to influence one or the masses, meaning "Always perform for one or for hundreds."

That little **Fremont Eagle basketball squad** that taught me how to actually live my life, and now you also have the power.

Jesus Christ: the ultimate Mark in Grace, Mercy, Humility, Ego, Empathy, Love, and Compassion. Even those who follow other higher powers will gain from this ultimate Mark.

Some of these Marks may seem small or even trivial, but they were defining moments for me and clearly acted upon my Supremely Purposeful mindset. They are proof of how important individuals play in our *Wired Differently* world of success.

Thanks again to these Marks.

ABOUT THE AUTHOR

Todd Saylor is a ferocious leader, and his persona is larger than life as his credits defy easy categorization: entrepreneur, CEO, football All-American, Manchester University Hall of Fame, inventor, talk-radio host, emcee, developer, donut-maker extraordinaire, and author of the book and brand *Wired Differently: Leveraging Your Favors on Fulcrum Principles*. He's also the Founder and President of PayServ Systems, one of the Payroll Service Bureau industry leaders in HR solutions. As Founder and Chairman of Call of America, a 501(c)(3) nonprofit organization, Saylor reached out to disadvantaged veterans to Feed, House, and Help Our Heroes. His lifetime of community church service includes speaker, teacher, elder, and deacon. His many accomplishments are overshadowed by his most important roles as a father, husband, and friend.

Made in the USA
Las Vegas, NV
10 February 2022

43637917R00085